WHAT'S COOKING
chicken

Tom Bridge

This edition published by Parragon, 1999
Parragon
Queen Street House
4 Queen Street
Bath BA1 1HE

Copyright © Dempsey Parr 1999

ISBN: 0-75252-939-0 (paperback)
ISBN: 0-75253-235-9 (hardback)

Printed in Indonesia

Produced by Haldane Mason, London

Acknowledgements
Art Director: Ron Samuels
Editorial Director: Sydney Francis
Managing Editor: Jo-Anne Cox
Editorial Assistant: Elizabeth Towers
Design: dap ltd
Photography: St John Asprey
Home Economist: Jacqueline Bellefontaine

The publishers would like to thank the British Chicken Information Service for
providing the recipes on pages 14–17, 38–41, 44, 48, 52, 58, 64, 70–75, 78–83,
88–93, 96–101, 104, 112, 116, 122, 130, 134, 138, 142, 148, 152–159, 162, 166,
170, 174–181, 184–187, 192–225, 228–233, 236–241, 244, 248–255

Note
Cup measurements in this book are for American cups.
Tablespoons are assumed to be 15 ml. Unless otherwise stated,
milk is assumed to be full fat, eggs are medium
and pepper is freshly ground black pepper.

Contents

Introduction

Chicken has become justly popular around the world and plays an important part in the modern diet, being reasonably priced and nutritionally sound. A versatile meat, it lends itself to an enormous range of cooking methods and cuisines. Its unassertive flavour means that it is equally suited to cooking with both sweet and savoury flavours. Because it has a low fat content, especially without the skin, it is an ideal meat for low cholesterol and calorie-controlled diets. As well as being an excellent source of protein, chicken contains valuable minerals, such as potassium and phosphorus, and some of the B vitamins.

COOKING METHODS FOR CHICKEN

Roasting Remove any fat from the body cavity. Rinse the bird inside and out with water, then pat dry with paper towels. Season the cavity generously with salt and pepper and add stuffing, herbs or lemon if wished. Spread the breast of the chicken with softened butter or oil. Set on a rack in a roasting tin (pan) or shallow baking dish. Roast the bird, basting two or three times with the pan juices during roasting. If the chicken is browning too quickly, cover it with foil. Test for doneness by using a meat thermometer or insert a skewer into the thickest part of the thigh. If the chicken is cooked, the juices will run clear with no trace of pink. Put the bird on a carving board and leave to rest for at least 15 minutes before serving. Make a sauce or gravy from the juices left in the roasting tin (pan).

Grilling (Broiling) The intense heat of the grill (broiler) quickly seals the succulent flesh beneath a crisp, golden exterior. Place the chicken 10–15 cm/4–6 inches away from a moderate heat source. If the chicken seems to be browning too quickly, reduce the heat slightly. If the chicken is grilled (broiled) at too high a temperature too near to the heat, the outside will burn before the inside is cooked. If it is cooked for too long under a low heat, it will dry out. Divide the chicken into joints to ensure even cooking. Breast meat, if cooked in one piece, can be rather dry, so it is best to cut it into chunks for kebabs (kabobs). Wings are best for speedy grilling (broiling).

Frying is suitable for small thighs, drumsticks and joints. Dry the chicken pieces with paper towels so that they brown properly and to prevent spitting during cooking. The chicken can be coated in seasoned flour, egg and breadcrumbs or a batter. Heat oil or a mixture of oil and butter in a heavy frying pan (skillet). When the oil is very hot, add the chicken pieces, skin-side down. Fry until deep golden brown all over, turning the pieces frequently during cooking. Drain well on paper towels before serving.

Sautéeing is ideal for small pieces or small birds such as baby chickens. Heat a little oil or a mixture of oil and butter in a heavy frying pan (skillet). Add the chicken and fry over a moderate heat until golden brown, turning frequently. Add stock or other liquid, bring to the boil, then cover and reduce the heat. Cook gently until the chicken is cooked through.

Stir-frying Skinless, boneless chicken is cut into small pieces of equal size to ensure that the meat cooks evenly and stays succulent. Preheat a wok or saucepan before adding a small amount of oil. When the oil starts to smoke, add the chicken and stir-fry with your chosen flavourings for 3–4 minutes until cooked through. Other ingredients can be cooked at the same time, or the chicken can be cooked by itself, then removed from the pan while you stir-fry the remaining ingredients. Return the chicken to the pan once the other ingredients are cooked.

Casseroling is good for cooking joints from larger, more mature chickens, although smaller chickens can be cooked whole. The slow cooking produces tender meat with a good flavour. Brown the chicken in butter or oil or a mixture of both. Add some stock, wine or a mixture of both with seasonings and herbs, cover and cook on top of the stove or in the oven until the chicken is tender. Add a selection of lightly sautéed vegetables about halfway through the cooking time.

Braising is a method which does not require liquid. The chicken pieces or a small whole chicken and vegetables are cooked together slowly in a low oven. Heat some oil in an ovenproof, flameproof casserole and gently fry the chicken until golden. Remove the chicken and fry a selection of vegetables until they are almost tender. Replace the chicken, cover tightly and cook very gently on the top of the stove or in a low oven until the chicken and vegetables are tender.

Poaching is a gentle cooking method that produces tender chicken and a stock that can be used to make a sauce to serve with the chicken. Put a whole chicken, a bouquet garni, a leek, a carrot and an onion in a large flameproof casserole. Cover with water, season and bring to the boil. Cover and simmer for $1\frac{1}{2}$–2 hours until the chicken is tender. Lift the chicken out, discard the bouquet garni and use the stock to make a sauce. The vegetables can be blended to thicken the stock and served with the chicken.

FOOD SAFETY & TIPS

Chicken is liable to be contaminated by salmonella bacteria, which can cause severe food poisoning. When storing, handling and preparing poultry, certain precautions must be observed to prevent the possibility of food poisoning.

● Check the sell-by date and best before date. After buying, take the chicken home quickly, preferably in a freezer bag or cool box.

● Return frozen birds immediately to the freezer.

● If storing in the refrigerator, remove the wrappings and store any giblets separately. Place the chicken in a shallow dish to catch drips. Cover loosely with foil and store on the bottom shelf of the refrigerator for no more than two or three days, depending on the best before date. Avoid any contact between raw chicken and cooked food during storage and preparation. Wash your hands thoroughly after handling raw chicken.

● Prepare raw chicken on a chopping board that can be easily cleaned and bleached, such as a non-porous, plastic board.

● Frozen birds should be defrosted before cooking. If time permits, defrost for about 36 hours in the refrigerator, or thaw for about 12 hours in a cool place. Bacteria breed in warm food at room temperature and when chicken is thawing. Cooking at high temperatures kills bacteria. There should be no ice crystals and the flesh should feel soft and flexible. Cook the chicken as soon as possible after thawing.

● Make sure that chicken is thoroughly cooked. Test for doneness using a meat thermometer – the thigh should reach at least 79°C/175°F when cooked – or pierce the thickest part of a thigh with a skewer, the juices should run clear, not pink or red. Never partially cook chicken with the intention of completing cooking later.

CHICKEN STOCK

Chicken stock is usually made from a whole bird or wings, backs and legs. This produces a well-flavoured stock. However it can also be made using chicken bones and carcass cooked with vegetables and flavourings. Although it will not be so rich in flavour it is still superior to stock make from a stock cube. A simple chicken stock can be made using giblets (except the liver which is bitter) with a bouquet garni, onion, carrot and some peppercorns. Home-made stock can be stored in the freezer for up to six months.

To make chicken stock: add the wings, backs or whole chicken to a large stockpot with two quartered onions. Cook until the chicken and onion are evenly browned. Cover with cold water, bring to the boil and skim off any skum that rises to the surface. Add two chopped carrots, two chopped celery sticks, a small bunch of parsley, a few bay leaves, a thyme sprig and a few peppercorns. Partially cover and gently simmer for about 3 hours. Strain the stock into a bowl and cool, then chill. When the stock is completely cold, remove the fat that will have set on the surface.

Soups & Snacks

Chicken soup has a long tradition of being comforting and good for us and some cultures even think of it as a cure for all ills. It is certainly satisfying, full of flavour and easy to digest. For the best results, use a good homemade chicken stock, although when time is at a premium, a good quality stock cube can be used instead. Every cuisine in the world has its own favourite version of chicken soup and in this section you'll find a selection of recipes from as far afield as Italy, Scotland and China.

As chicken is so versatile and quick to cook, it is perfect for innovative and appetizing snacks. Its unassertive flavour means that it can be enlivened by exotic fruits and spices and oriental ingredients, such as mirin, sesame oil and fresh ginger root. There are fritters, salads, and drumsticks that are stuffed and baked, or served with delicious fruity salsas. Because chicken pieces travel well and are easy to eat, many of the recipes are ideal to take on picnics or to pack into a lunch box.

Cream of Chicken & Lemon Soup

This refreshing soup with its refreshing lemon flavour
is perfect on summer days.

Serves 4

INGREDIENTS

60 g/2 oz/4 tbsp butter
8 shallots, sliced thinly
2 medium carrots, sliced thinly
2 stalks celery, sliced thinly
250 g/9 oz skinless chicken breast
    meat, chopped finely

3 lemons
1.2 litres/2 pints/5 cups chicken stock
150 ml/$^{1}/_{4}$ pint/$^{2}/_{3}$ cup double
    (heavy) cream
salt and pepper

sprigs of parsley and lemon slices,
    to garnish

1 Melt the butter in a large saucepan, add the vegetables and chicken and cook gently for 8 minutes.

2 Thinly pare the lemons and blanch the lemon rind in boiling water for 3 minutes.

3 Squeeze the juice from the lemons.

4 Add the lemon rind and freshly squeezed lemon juice to the pan with the chicken stock.

5 Bring slowly to the boil and simmer for about 50 minutes. Leave the soup to cool then transfer to a food processor and blend until smooth. Return the soup to the saucepan, reheat, season with salt and pepper to taste and add the double (heavy) cream. Do not boil at this stage or the soup will curdle.

6 Transfer the soup to a tureen or warm individual bowls. Serve, garnished with parsley and lemon slices.

VARIATION

For an alternative citrus flavour, use 4 oranges in place of the lemons. The recipe can also be adapted to make duck and orange soup.

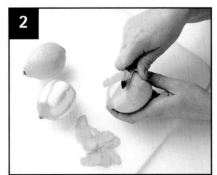

Tom's Chicken Soup

The potato has been part of the Irish diet for centuries. This recipe is originally from the north of Ireland, in the beautiful area of Moira, County Down.

Serves 4

INGREDIENTS

3 smoked, streaky,
  rindless bacon slices, chopped
500 g/1 lb 2 oz boneless chicken,
  chopped
25 g/1 oz/2 tbsp butter
3 medium potatoes, chopped

3 medium onions, chopped
600 ml/1 pint/2^{1}/$_2$ cups giblet or
  chicken stock
600 ml/1 pint/2^{1}/$_2$ cups milk
150 ml/^{1}/$_4$ pint/^{2}/$_3$ cup double
  (heavy) cream

salt and pepper
2 tbsp chopped fresh parsley
soda bread, to serve

1 Gently fry the bacon and chicken in a large saucepan for 10 minutes.

2 Add the butter, potatoes and onions and cook for 15 minutes, stirring all the time.

3 Add the stock and milk, then bring the soup to the boil and simmer for 45 minutes. Season with salt and pepper to taste.

4 Blend in the cream and simmer for 5 minutes. Stir in the chopped fresh parsley, then transfer the soup to a warm tureen or individual bowls and serve with Irish soda bread.

COOK'S TIP

Soda bread is not made with yeast as bread usually is. Instead it is made with bicarbonate of soda as the raising agent. It can be made with plain (all-purpose) flour or wholemeal (whole wheat) flour.

VARIATION

For a more filling, main course soup, you can add any number of different vegetables, for example leeks, celeriac (celery root) or sweetcorn.

Chicken & Leek Soup

This satisfying soup can be served as a main course.
You can add rice and (bell) peppers to make it even more hearty, as well as colourful.

Serves 6

INGREDIENTS

350 g/12 oz boneless chicken
350 g/12 oz leeks
30 g/1 oz/2 tbsp butter
1.2 litres/2 pints/5 cups chicken stock

1 bouquet garni sachet
8 pitted prunes, halved
salt and white pepper

cooked rice and diced (bell) peppers
(optional)

1 Using a sharp knife, cut the chicken and leeks into 2.5-cm/1-inch pieces.

2 Melt the butter in a large saucepan, add the chicken and leeks and fry for 8 minutes, stirring occasionally.

3 Add the chicken stock and bouquet garni sachet to the mixture in the pan, and season with salt and pepper to taste.

4 Bring the soup to the boil and simmer over a gentle heat for 45 minutes.

5 Add the pitted prunes with some cooked rice and diced (bell) peppers (if using), and simmer for 20 minutes. Remove the bouquet garni sachet and discard. Pour the soup into a warm tureen or individual bowls and serve.

COOK'S TIP

If you have time, make the chicken stock yourself, using the recipe on page 5. Alternatively, you can buy good fresh stock from supermarkets.

COOK'S TIP

Instead of the bouquet garni sachet, you can use a bunch of fresh, mixed herbs, tied together with string. Choose herbs such as parsley, thyme and rosemary.

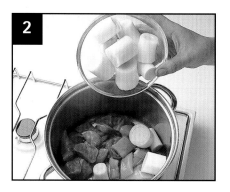

Thai Chicken Noodle Soup

Quick to make, this hot and spicy soup is hearty and warming. If you like your food really fiery, add a chopped dried or fresh chilli with its seeds.

Serves 4–6

INGREDIENTS

1 sheet of dried egg noodles
   from a 250 g/9 oz pack
1 tbsp oil
4 skinless, boneless
   chicken thighs, diced
1 bunch spring onions
   (scallions), sliced
2 garlic cloves, chopped

2 cm/^{3}/$_4$ inch piece fresh
   ginger root, finely chopped
850 ml/1^1/$_2$ pints/3^3/$_4$ cups
   chicken stock
200 ml/7 fl oz/scant 1 cup
   coconut milk
3 tsp red Thai curry paste
3 tbsp peanut butter

2 tbsp light soy sauce
1 small red (bell) pepper,
   chopped
60 g/2 oz/^{1}/$_2$ cup frozen peas
salt and pepper

1 Put the noodles in a shallow dish and soak in boiling water following the instructions on the packet.

2 Heat the oil in a large saucepan or wok, add the chicken, and fry for 5 minutes, stirring until lightly browned. Add the white part of the spring onions (scallions), the garlic and ginger and fry for 2 minutes, stirring. Add the stock, coconut milk, curry paste, peanut butter and soy sauce. Season with salt and pepper to taste. Bring to the boil, stirring, then simmer for 8 minutes, stirring occasionally. Add the red (bell) pepper, peas and green spring onion (scallion) tops and cook for 2 minutes.

3 Add the drained noodles and heat through. Spoon into individual bowls and serve with a spoon and fork.

VARIATION

Green Thai curry paste can be used instead of red curry paste for a less fiery flavour.

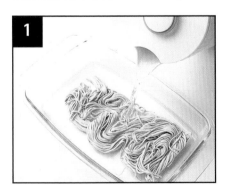

Chicken & Pasta Broth

This satisfying soup makes a good lunch or supper dish and you can use any vegetables that you have at hand. Children will love the tiny pasta shapes.

Serves 6

INGREDIENTS

350 g/12 oz boneless
  chicken breasts
2 tbsp sunflower oil
1 medium onion, diced
250 g/9 oz/1^1/2 cups carrots, diced
250 g/9 oz cauliflower florets

850 ml/1^1/2 pints/3^3/4 cups
  chicken stock
2 tsp dried mixed herbs
125 g/4^1/2 oz small pasta shapes
salt and pepper

Parmesan cheese (optional)
  and crusty bread, to serve

1 Using a sharp knife, finely dice the chicken, discarding any skin.

2 Heat the oil in a large saucepan and quickly sauté the chicken and vegetables until they are lightly coloured.

3 Stir in the stock and herbs. Bring to the boil and add the pasta shapes. Return to the boil, cover and simmer for 10 minutes, stirring occasionally to prevent the pasta shapes sticking together.

4 Season with salt and pepper to taste and sprinkle with Parmesan cheese, if using. Serve with fresh crusty bread.

COOK'S TIP

You can use any small pasta shapes for this soup – try conchigliette or ditalini or even spaghetti broken up into small pieces. To make a fun soup for children you could add animal-shaped or alphabet pasta.

VARIATION

Broccoli florets can be used to replace the cauliflower florets. Substitute 2 tablespoons chopped fresh mixed herbs for the dried mixed herbs.

Chicken Consommé

This is a very flavourful soup, especially if you make it from real chicken stock.
Egg shells are used to give a crystal clear appearance.

Serves 8-10

INGREDIENTS

1.75 litres/3 pints/8 cups chicken
   stock
150 ml/$^1/_4$ pint/$^2/_3$ cup medium
   sherry

4 egg whites plus egg shells
125 g/4 oz cooked chicken, sliced
   thinly
salt and pepper

1 Place the chicken stock and sherry in a large saucepan and heat gently for 5 minutes.

2 Add the egg whites and the egg shells to the chicken stock and whisk until the mixture begins to boil.

3 Remove the pan from the heat and allow the mixture to subside for 10 minutes. Repeat this process three times. This allows the egg white to trap the sediments in the chicken stock to clarify the soup. Let the consommé cool for 5 minutes.

4 Carefully place a piece of fine muslin (cheesecloth) over a clean saucepan. Ladle the soup over the muslin and strain into the saucepan.

5 Repeat this process twice, then gently re-heat the consommé. Season with salt and pepper to taste then add the cooked chicken slices. Pour the soup into a warm serving dish or individual bowls.

6 Garnish the consommé with any of the suggestions in the Cook's Tip, right.

COOK'S TIP

Consommé is usually garnished with freshly cooked pasta shapes, noodles, rice or lightly cooked vegetables. Alternatively, you could garnish it with omelette strips, drained first on paper towels.

Chicken Mulligatawny Soup

*This spicy soup was brought to the west by army
and service personnel returning from India.*

Serves 4

INGREDIENTS

60 g/2 oz/4 tbsp butter
1 onion, sliced
1 garlic clove, crushed
500 g/1 lb 2 oz chicken, diced
60 g/2 oz/$^1/_3$ cup smoked rindless
   bacon, diced
1 small turnip, diced
2 carrots, diced

1 small cooking apple, diced
2 tbsp mild curry powder
1 tbsp curry paste
1 tbsp tomato purée (paste)
1 tbsp plain (all-purpose) flour
1.2 litres/2 pints/5 cups chicken stock
150 ml/$^1/_4$ pint/$^2/_3$ cup double
   (heavy) cream

salt and pepper
1 tsp of chopped fresh
   coriander (cilantro), to garnish

1 Melt the butter in a large saucepan and cook the onion, garlic, chicken and bacon for 5 minutes.

2 Add the turnip, carrots and apple and cook for a further two minutes.

3 Blend in the curry powder, curry paste and tomato purée (paste), and sprinkle over the plain (all-purpose) flour.

4 Add the chicken stock and bring to the boil, cover and simmer over a gentle heat for about 1 hour.

5 Liquidize the soup. Reheat, season well with salt and pepper to taste and gradually blend in the double (heavy) cream. Garnish the soup with chopped fresh coriander (cilantro) and serve over small bowls of boiled or fried rice.

COOK'S TIP

This soup may be frozen for up to 1 month; if stored for any longer, the spices may cause it to taste musty.

Chicken & Pea Soup

A hearty soup that is so simple to make yet packed with flavour.
You can use either whole green peas or green or yellow split peas.

Serves 4–6

INGREDIENTS

3 smoked, streaky, rindless bacon
  slices, chopped
900 g/2 lb chicken, chopped
1 large onion, chopped
15 g/^{1}/2 oz/1 tbsp butter
500 g/1 lb 2 oz/2^1/2 cups ready-
  soaked peas

2.4 litres/4 pints/10 cups chicken
  stock
150 ml/^{1}/4 pint/^{2}/3 cup double
  (heavy) cream
2 tbsp chopped fresh parsley

salt and pepper
cheesy croûtes, to garnish

1 Put the bacon, chicken and onion into a large saucepan with a little butter and cook over a gentle heat for 8 minutes.

2 Add the peas and the stock to the pan, bring to the boil, season lightly with salt and pepper, cover and simmer for 2 hours.

3 Blend the double (heavy) cream into the soup, sprinkle with parsley and top with cheesy croûtes (see Cook's Tip, right).

COOK'S TIP

Croûtes are slices of French bread that are fried or baked, then they can be sprinkled with grated cheese and lightly toasted.

VARIATION

Use 100 g/3^1/2 oz chopped ham instead of the bacon, if you prefer.

COOK'S TIP

If using dried peas, soak them for several hours or overnight in a large bowl of cold water. Alternatively, bring them to the boil in a pan of cold water. Remove from the heat and leave to cool in the water. Drain and rinse the beans before adding them to the soup.

Cream of Chicken Soup

Tarragon adds a delicate aniseed flavour to this tasty soup.
If you can't find tarragon, use parsley for a fresh taste.

Serves 4

INGREDIENTS

60 g/2 oz/4 tbsp unsalted butter
1 large onion, peeled and chopped
300 g/10^1/$_2$ oz cooked chicken,
   shredded finely
600 ml/1 pint/2^1/$_2$ cups chicken stock
1 tbsp chopped fresh tarragon

150 ml/^{1}/$_4$ pint/^{2}/$_3$ cup double
   (heavy) cream
salt and pepper
fresh tarragon leaves, to garnish
deep fried croûtons, to serve

1 Melt the butter in a large saucepan and fry the onion for 3 minutes.

2 Add the chicken to the pan with 300 ml/½ pint/1¼ cups of the chicken stock.

3 Bring to the boil and simmer for 20 minutes. Allow to cool, then liquidize the soup.

4 Add the remainder of the stock and season with salt and pepper.

5 Add the chopped tarragon, pour the soup into a tureen or individual serving bowls and add a swirl of cream.

6 Garnish the soup with fresh tarragon and serve with deep fried croûtons.

VARIATION

To make garlic croûtons, crush 3–4 garlic cloves in a pestle and mortar and add to the oil.

VARIATION

If you can't find fresh tarragon, freeze-dried tarragon makes a good substitute. Single (light) cream can be used instead of the double (heavy) cream.

Chicken Soup with Coriander (Cilantro) Dumplings

Use the strained vegetables and chicken to make little patties. Simply mash with a little butter, shape them into round cakes and fry in butter or oil until golden brown.

Serves 6–8

INGREDIENTS

900 g/2 lb chicken meat, sliced
60 g/2 oz/¹/₂ cup plain (all-purpose) flour
125 g/4¹/₂ oz/¹/₂ cup butter
3 tbsp sunflower oil
1 large carrot, chopped
1 stick (stalk) celery, chopped
1 onion, chopped
1 small turnip, chopped

120 ml/4 fl oz/¹/₂ cup sherry
1 tsp thyme
1 bay leaf
1.75 litres/3 pints/8 cups chicken stock
salt and pepper
crusty bread, to serve

DUMPLINGS:
60 g/2 oz/¹/₂ cup self-raising flour
60 g/2 oz/1 cup fresh breadcrumbs
2 tbsp shredded suet
2 tbsp chopped fresh coriander (cilantro)
2 tbsp finely grated lemon rind
1 egg
salt and pepper

1 Coat the chicken pieces with the flour and season.

2 Melt the butter in a saucepan and fry the chicken pieces until they are lightly browned.

3 Add the oil to the pan and brown the vegetables. Add the sherry and the remaining ingredients except the stock.

4 Cook for 10 minutes, then add the stock. Simmer for 3 hours, then strain into a clean saucepan and allow to cool.

5 To make the dumplings, mix together all the dry ingredients in a large clean bowl. Add the egg and blend in thoroughly then add enough milk to make a moist dough.

6 Shape into small balls and roll them in a little flour.

7 Cook the dumplings in boiling salted water for 10 minutes.

8 Remove them carefully with a slotted spoon and add them to the soup. Cook for a further 12 minutes, then serve.

Dickensian Chicken Broth

This soup is made with traditional Scottish ingredients. It should be left for at least two days before being re-heated, then served with oatmeal cakes or bread.

Serves 4

INGREDIENTS

60 g/2 oz/^{1}/$_3$ cup
  pre-soaked dried peas
900 g/2 lb diced chicken,
  fat removed
1.2 litres/2 pints/5 cups chicken stock
600 ml/1 pint/2^1/$_2$ cups water

60 g/2 oz/^{1}/$_4$ cup barley
1 large carrot, peeled and diced
1 small turnip, peeled and diced
1 large leek, thinly sliced
1 red onion, chopped finely
salt and white pepper

1 Put the peas and chicken into a pan, add the stock and water and bring slowly to the boil.

2 Skim the stock as it boils using a slotted spoon.

3 When all the scum is removed, add the washed barley and salt and simmer for 35 minutes.

4 Add the remaining ingredients and simmer for 2 hours.

5 Skim the surface of the soup again and allow the broth to stand for at least 24 hours. Reheat, adjust the seasoning and serve.

VARIATION

This soup is just as delicious made with beef or lamb. Substitute 225 g/8 oz lean sirloin beef or lean lamb fillet for the chicken. Trim any fat from the meat and cut into thin strips before using.

COOK'S TIP

Use either whole grain barley or pearl barley. Only the outer husk is removed from whole grain barley and when cooked it has a nutty flavour and a chewy texture.

Cream of Chicken & Orange Soup

*For a tangy flavour, lemons can be used instead of oranges and the recipe
can be adapted to make duck and orange soup.*

Serves 4

INGREDIENTS

60 g/2 oz/4 tbsp butter
8 shallots, sliced thinly
2 medium carrots, sliced thinly
2 sticks (stalks) celery,
   sliced thinly

250 g/8 oz skinless chicken breast,
   chopped finely
3 oranges
1.2 litres/2 pints/5 cups chicken stock
150 ml/$^1/_4$ pint/$^2/_3$ cup double
   (heavy) cream

salt and white pepper
sprig of parsley and 3 orange slices,
   to garnish

1 Melt the butter in a large saucepan, add the shallots, carrot, celery and chicken meat and cook gently for 8 minutes, stirring occasionally.

2 Using a potato peeler or sharp knife, thinly pare the oranges and blanch the rind in boiling water for about 3 minutes.

3 Squeeze the juice from the oranges. Add the orange rind and orange juice to the pan together with the chicken stock.

4 Bring slowly to the boil and simmer for 50 minutes. Cool the soup then liquidize in a blender or food processor until smooth.

5 Return the soup to the saucepan, reheat, season to taste and add the cream. Do not boil at this stage or the soup will curdle.

6 Transfer the soup to a serving dish or individual bowls. Garnish with a sprig of parsley, orange slices and serve with soda bread.

VARIATION

Use 2 small lemons in place of the oranges. Look for organic or unwaxed lemons when using rind.

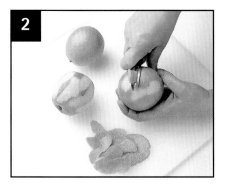

Chicken, Guinea Fowl & Spaghetti Soup

Guinea fowl has a similar texture to chicken, and although it has a milder flavour than other game, it has a slightly gamier flavour than chicken.

Serves 6

INGREDIENTS

500 g/1 lb 2 oz skinless chicken, chopped
500 g/1 lb 2 oz skinless guinea fowl meat
600 ml/1 pint/2¹/₂ cups chicken stock
1 small onion

6 peppercorns
1 tsp cloves
pinch of mace
150 ml/¹/₄ pint/²/₃ cup double (heavy) cream
2 tsp butter

2 tsp plain (all-purpose) flour
125 g/4¹/₂ oz/1 cup quick-cook spaghetti, broken into short lengths and cooked
2 tbsp chopped fresh parsley, to garnish

1 Put the chicken and guinea fowl meat into a large saucepan with the chicken stock.

2 Bring to the boil and add the onion, peppercorns, cloves and mace. Simmer gently for about 2 hours until the stock is reduced by one-third.

3 Strain the soup, skim off any fat and remove any bones from the chicken and guinea fowl.

4 Return the soup and meat to a clean saucepan. Add the double (heavy) cream and bring to the boil slowly.

5 To make a roux, melt the butter and stir in the flour until it has a paste-like consistency. Add to the soup, stirring until slightly thickened.

6 Just before serving, add the cooked quick-cook spaghetti.

7 Transfer the soup to individual serving bowls, garnish with parsley and serve.

VARIATION

Instead of spaghetti, use small pasta shapes such as ziti or macaroni.

Cream of Chicken & Tomato Soup

This soup is very good made wih fresh tomatoes,
but if you prefer, you can use canned tomatoes.

Serves 2

INGREDIENTS

60 g/2 oz/4 tbsp unsalted butter
1 large onion, chopped
500 g/1 lb 2 oz chicken,
   shredded very finely
600 ml/1 pint/2¹/₂ cups chicken stock
6 medium tomatoes, chopped finely

pinch of bicarbonate of soda
   (baking soda)
1 tbsp caster (superfine) sugar
150 ml/1¹/₄ pint/²/₃ cup double
   (heavy) cream
salt and pepper

fresh basil leaves, to garnish
croûtons, to serve

1 Melt the butter in a large saucepan and fry the onion and shredded chicken for 5 minutes.

2 Add 300 ml/¹/₂ pint/1¹/₄ cups chicken stock to the pan, with the tomatoes and bicarbonate of soda (baking soda).

3 Bring the soup to the boil and simmer for 20 minutes.

4 Allow the soup to cool, then blend in a food processor.

5 Return the soup to the pan, add the remaining chicken stock, season and add the sugar. Pour the soup into a tureen and add a swirl of double (heavy) cream. Serve the soup with croûtons and garnish with basil.

COOK'S TIP

For a healthier version of this soup, use single (light) cream instead of the double (heavy) cream and omit the sugar.

VARIATION

For an Italian-style soup, add 1 tbsp chopped fresh basil with the stock in step 2. Alternatively, add ¹/₂ tsp curry powder or chilli powder to make a spicier version of this soup.

Chicken Wonton Soup

*This Chinese-style soup is delicious as a starter
to an oriental meal or as a light meal.*

Serves 4-6

INGREDIENTS

FILLING:
350 g/12 oz minced (ground) chicken
1 tbsp soy sauce
1 tsp grated, fresh ginger root
1 garlic clove, crushed
2 tsp sherry
2 spring onions (scallions), chopped

1 tsp sesame oil
1 egg white
$^1/_2$ tsp cornflour (cornstarch)
$^1/_2$ tsp sugar
about 35 wonton wrappers

SOUP:
1.5 litres/$2^3/_4$ pints/6 cups chicken
  stock
1 tbsp light soy sauce
1 spring onion (scallion), shredded
1 small carrot, cut into
  very thin slices

1 Combine all the ingredients for the filling and mix well.

2 Place a small spoonful of the filling in the centre of each wonton wrapper.

3 Dampen the edges and gather up the wonton wrapper to form a pouch enclosing the filling.

4 Cook the filled wontons in boiling water for 1 minute or until they float to the top.

5 Remove with a slotted spoon. Bring the chicken stock to the boil.

6 Add the soy sauce, spring onion (scallion), carrot and wontons to the soup. Simmer gently for 2 minutes then serve.

VARIATION

*Substitute the chicken for minced
(ground) pork.*

COOK'S TIP

*Look for wonton wrappers in
Chinese or oriental supermarkets.
Fresh wrappers can be found in the
chilled compartment and they can
be frozen if you wish. Wrap
in cling film (plastic wrap)
before freezing.*

Chicken & Cheese Jackets

Use the breasts from a roasted chicken for this delicious, healthy snack. Served with a mixed salad,
it is an ideal light meal for a summer's day.

Serves 4

INGREDIENTS

4 large baking potatoes
250 g/9 oz cooked, boneless
   chicken breasts
4 spring onions (scallions)

250 g/9 oz/1 cup low-fat
   soft cheese or Quark
pepper

coleslaw, green salad or a mixed
   salad, to serve

1 Scrub the potatoes and prick them all over with a fork. Bake in a preheated oven, 200°C/400°F/Gas Mark 6, for about 50 minutes until tender, or cook in a microwave on High/ 100% power for 12–15 minutes.

2 Using a sharp knife, dice the chicken, trim and thickly slice the spring onions (scallions) and mix with the low-fat soft cheese or Quark.

3 Cut a cross through the top of each potato and pull slightly apart. Spoon the chicken filling into the potatoes and sprinkle with freshly ground black pepper. Serve immediately with coleslaw, green salad or a mixed salad.

VARIATION

For another delicious filling, fry 250 g/9 oz button mushrooms in a little butter. Mix with the chicken then add 150 g/5¹/₂ oz/²/₃ cup natural (unsweetened) yogurt, 1 tbsp tomato purée (paste) and 2 tsp mild curry powder. Blend well and use to fill the jackets.

COOK'S TIP

Look for Quark in the chilled section. It is a low-fat, white, fresh curd cheese made from cow's milk with a delicate, slightly sour flavour.

Sticky Chicken Drummers with Mango Salsa

Delicious served hot or cold, and any leftover chicken can be packed in lunchboxes for a tasty alternative to sandwiches.

Serves 4

INGREDIENTS

8 skinless chicken drumsticks
3 tbsp mango chutney
2 tsp Dijon mustard
2 tsp oil
1 tsp paprika
1 tsp black mustard seeds,
　roughly crushed

$1/2$ tsp turmeric
2 garlic cloves, chopped
salt and pepper

SALSA:
1 mango, diced
1 tomato, chopped finely

$1/2$ red onion, sliced thinly
2 tbsp chopped fresh coriander
　(cilantro)

1 Using a small, sharp knife, slash each drumstick three or four times then place in a roasting tin (pan).

2 In a small bowl, mix together the mango chutney, mustard, oil, spices, garlic and salt and pepper and spoon over the chicken drumsticks, turning until they are coated all over with the glaze.

3 Cook in a preheated oven, 200°C/ 400°F/Gas Mark 6, for 40 minutes, brushing with the glaze several times during cooking until the chicken is well browned and the juices run clear when pierced with a skewer.

4 To make the salsa, combine the mango, tomato, onion and coriander (cilantro). Season to taste and chill until required.

5 Arrange the chicken drumsticks on a serving plate and serve hot or cold with the mango salsa.

VARIATION

Use mild curry powder instead of the turmeric.

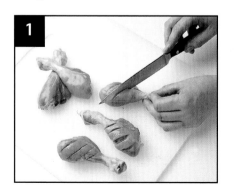

Open Chicken Sandwiches

These tasty sandwiches are good as a snack on their own or they can be served as part of a picnic spread.

Serves 6

INGREDIENTS

6 thick slices of bread or a large French stick cut lengthways, then cut into 6 pieces and buttered
3 hard-boiled (hard-cooked) eggs, the yolk sieved & the white chopped

25 g/1 oz/2 tbsp butter, softened
2 tbsp English mustard
1 tsp anchovy essence (extract)
250 g/9 oz/2 cups grated Cheddar cheese
3 cooked, skinless chicken breasts, chopped finely

12 slices each of tomato and cucumber
pepper

1 Remove the crusts from the bread (optional).

2 Reserve the yolk and the white separately from 1 egg.

3 In a large bowl, mix the remaining egg with the softened butter, English mustard and anchovy essence (extract) and season well with pepper.

4 Mix in the grated Cheddar cheese and chicken and spread the mixture on the bread.

5 Make alternate rows of the egg yolk and the egg white on top of the chicken mixture. Arrange the tomato and cucumber slices on top of the egg and serve.

COOK'S TIP

To soften butter, let it stand at room temperature for 30 minutes or, if you are short of time, cream it in a bowl with a fork. Alternatively, there are now varieties of soft butter available from supermarkets.

COOK'S TIP

If you prefer a less spicy flavour, use a milder mustard. Add mayonnaise if wished and garnish with watercress.

VARIATION

Add 50 g/1¾ oz finely chopped grilled (broiled) bacon to the chicken and cheese mixture for a crunchier texture.

Chicken Pepperonata

All the sunshine colours and flavours of the Mediterranean are combined in this easy dish.

Serves 4

INGREDIENTS

8 skinless chicken thighs
2 tbsp wholemeal
   (whole wheat) flour
2 tbsp olive oil
1 small onion, sliced thinly
1 garlic clove, crushed

1 each large red, yellow and green
   (bell) peppers, sliced thinly
400 g/14 oz can chopped tomatoes
1 tbsp chopped oregano
salt and pepper
fresh oregano, to garnish

crusty wholemeal (whole wheat)
   bread, to serve

1 Remove the skin from the chicken thighs and toss in the flour.

2 Heat the oil in a wide pan and fry the chicken quickly until sealed and lightly browned, then remove from the pan. Add the onion to the pan and gently fry until soft. Add the garlic, (bell) peppers, tomatoes and oregano, then bring to the boil, stirring.

3 Arrange the chicken over the vegetables, season well with salt and pepper, then cover the pan tightly and simmer for 20–25 minutes or until the chicken is completely cooked and tender.

4 Season to taste, garnish with oregano and serve with crusty wholemeal (whole wheat) bread.

COOK'S TIP

If you do not have fresh oregano, use canned tomatoes with herbs already added.

COOK'S TIP

For extra flavour, halve the peppers and grill (broil) under a preheated grill (broiler) until the skins are charred. Leave to cool then remove the skins and seeds. Slice the (bell) peppers thinly and use in the recipe.

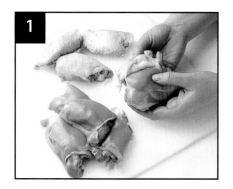

Chicken & Herb Fritters

These fritters are delicious served with a green salad,
a fresh vegetable salsa or a chilli sauce dip.

Makes 8

INGREDIENTS

500 g/1 lb 2 oz mashed potato,
   with butter added
250 g/9 oz/1^1/$_3$ cups chopped,
   cooked chicken
125 g/4^1/$_2$ oz/^{2}/$_3$ cups cooked ham,
   chopped finely

1 tbsp mixed herbs
2 eggs, lightly beaten
milk
125 g/4^1/$_2$ oz/2 cups fresh brown
   breadcrumbs
oil for shallow frying

salt and pepper
sprig of fresh parsley, to garnish
mixed salad, to serve

1 In a large bowl, blend the potatoes, chicken, ham, herbs and 1 egg, and season well.

2 Shape the mixture into small balls or flat pancakes.

3 Add a little milk to the second egg.

4 Place the breadcrumbs on a plate. Dip the balls in the egg and milk mixture then roll in the breadcrumbs, to coat them completely.

5 Heat the cooking oil in a large frying pan (skillet) and cook the fritters until they are golden brown. Garnish with a sprig of fresh parsley and serve with a mixed salad.

COOK'S TIP

A mixture of chopped fresh tarragon and parsley makes a fresh and flavourful addition to these fritters.

COOK'S TIP

To make a tomato sauce to serve with the fritters, heat 200 ml/7 fl oz/^{3}/$_4$ cup passata (sieved tomatoes) and 4 tbsp dry white wine. Season, remove from the heat and add 4 tbsp natural (unsweetened) yogurt. Return to the heat and add chilli powder to taste.

Oaty Chicken Pieces

A very low-fat chicken recipe with a refreshingly light, mustard-spiced sauce, which is ideal for a healthy lunchbox or a light meal with salad.

Serves 4

INGREDIENTS

25 g/1 oz/^{1}/$_3$ cup rolled oats
1 tbsp chopped fresh rosemary
4 skinless chicken quarters
1 egg white
150 g/5^1/$_2$ oz/^{1}/$_2$ cup natural
   low-fat fromage frais

2 tsp wholegrain mustard
salt and pepper
grated carrot salad, to serve

1 Mix together the rolled oats, fresh rosemary and salt and pepper.

2 Brush each piece of chicken evenly with egg white, then coat in the oat mixture. Place on a baking sheet and bake in a preheated oven, 200°C/400°F/Gas Mark 6, for about 40 minutes or until the juices run clear when the chicken is pierced.

3 In a bowl, mix together the fromage frais and wholegrain mustard, season with salt and pepper to taste then serve with the chicken, hot or cold, with a grated carrot salad.

VARIATION

To make oaty chicken nuggets, chop up 4 skinless, boneless chicken breasts into small pieces. Reduce the cooking time by about 10 minutes and test for doneness. These nuggets would be ideal at a picnic, buffet or children's party.

VARIATION

Add 1 tablespoon sesame or sunflower seeds to the oat mixture for an even crunchier texture. Experiment with different herbs, instead of the rosemary.

Solomongundy

This recipe is ideally suited as a cold platter for a buffet party or a spectacular starter for a special meal.

Serves 4

INGREDIENTS

1 large lettuce

4 chicken breasts,
   cooked and sliced thinly

8 rollmop herrings and
   their marinade

6 hard-boiled (hard-cooked) eggs,
   quartered

125 g/4^1/2 oz/^{2}/3 cup cooked ham,
   sliced

125 g/4^1/2 oz/2^2/3 cups roast beef,
   sliced

125 g/4^1/2 oz/^{2}/3 cup roast lamb,
   sliced

150 g/5^1/2 oz/1 cup mangetout
   (snow peas), cooked

125 g/4^1/2 oz/^{3}/4 cup seedless black
   grapes,

20 stuffed olives, sliced

12 shallots, boiled

60 g/2 oz/^{1}/2 cup flaked (slivered)
   almonds

60 g/2 oz/^{1}/3 cup sultanas
   (golden raisins)

2 oranges

sprig of mint

salt and pepper

fresh crusty bread, to serve

1 Spread out the lettuce leaves on a large oval platter.

2 Arrange the chicken in three sections on the platter.

3 Place the roll mops, eggs and meats in lines or sections over the remainder of the platter.

4 Use the mangetout (snow peas), grapes, olives, shallots, almonds and sultanas (golden raisins) to fill in the spaces between the sections.

5 Grate the rind from the oranges and sprinkle over the whole platter. Peel and slice the oranges and add the orange slices and mint sprig to the platter. Season well with salt and pepper. Sprinkle with the herring marinade and serve.

VARIATION

Should you wish, serve with cold, cooked vegetables, such as sliced beans, baby sweetcorn (corn-on-the-cob) and cooked beetroot (beets).

Chicken Pan Bagna

*Perfect for a picnic or packed lunch, this Mediterranean-style
sandwich can be prepared in advance.*

Serves 6

INGREDIENTS

1 large French stick
1 garlic clove
125 ml/4 fl oz/^{1}/$_2$ cup olive oil
20 g/^{3}/$_4$ oz canned anchovy fillets

50 g/2 oz cold roast chicken
2 large tomatoes, sliced
8 large, pitted black olives, chopped
pepper

1 Using a sharp bread knife, cut the French stick in half lengthways and open out.

2 Cut the garlic clove in half and rub over the bread.

3 Sprinkle the cut surface of the bread with the olive oil.

4 Drain the anchovies and set aside.

5 Thinly slice the chicken and arrange on top of the bread. Arrange the tomatoes and drained anchovies on top of the chicken.

6 Scatter with the chopped black olives and plenty of black pepper. Sandwich the loaf back together and wrap tightly in foil until required. Cut into slices to serve.

VARIATION

*You could use Italian ciabatta or
olive-studded focaccia bread instead
of the French stick, if you prefer.
The last few years have seen a
veritable interest in different breads
and supermarkets now stock a wide
range from home and abroad.*

COOK'S TIP

*Arrange a few fresh basil leaves in
between the tomato slices to add a
warm, spicy flavour.
Use a good quality
olive oil in this recipe
for extra flavour.*

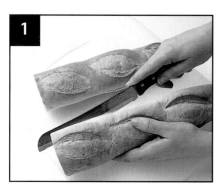

Coronation Chicken

This classic salad is good as a starter or as part of a buffet.
Mango chutney makes a tasty addition.

Serves 6

INGREDIENTS

4 tbsp olive oil
900 g/2 lb chicken meat, diced
125 g/4^{1}/$_{2}$ oz/^{2}/$_{3}$ cup rindless,
   smoked bacon, diced
12 shallots
2 garlic cloves, crushed

1 tbsp mild curry powder
300 ml/^{1}/$_{2}$ pint/1^{1}/$_{4}$ cups mayonnaise
1 tbsp runny honey
1 tbsp chopped fresh parsley
90 g/3 oz/^{1}/$_{2}$ cup seedless black
   grapes, quartered

pepper
cold saffron rice, to serve

1 Heat the oil in a large frying pan (skillet) and add the chicken, bacon, shallots, garlic and curry powder. Cook slowly for about 15 minutes.

2 Spoon the mixture into a clean mixing bowl.

3 Allow the mixture to cool completely then season with pepper to taste.

4 Blend the mayonnaise with a little honey, then add the chopped fresh parsley. Toss the chicken in the mixture.

5 Place the mixture in a deep serving dish, garnish with the grapes and serve with cold saffron rice.

COOK'S TIP

You can use this recipe to fill a jacket potato or as a sandwich filling, but cut the chicken into smaller pieces.

VARIATION

Add 2 tbsp chopped fresh apricots and 2 tbsp flaked (slivered) almonds to the sauce in step 4. For a healthier version of this dish, replace the mayonnaise with the same quantity of natural (unsweetened) yogurt and omit the honey otherwise the sauce will be too runny.

Potted Smoked Chicken

This recipe can be made a few days ahead and kept chilled until needed. A food processor makes light work of blending the ingredients, but you can pound by hand for a coarser mixture.

Serves 4-6

INGREDIENTS

350 g/12 oz/2$^1/_2$ cups
  chopped smoked chicken
pinch each of grated nutmeg and
  mace

125 g/4$^1/_2$ oz/$^1/_2$ cup butter, softened
2 tbsp port
2 tbsp double (heavy) cream
salt and pepper

sprig of fresh parsley, to garnish
brown bread slices and fresh butter,
  to serve

1 Place the smoked chicken in a large bowl with the remaining ingredients, and season with salt and pepper to taste.

2 Pound until the mixture is very smooth or blend in a food processor.

3 Transfer the mixture to individual earthenware pots or one large pot.

4 Cover each pot with buttered baking parchment and weigh down with cans or weights. Chill in the refrigerator for 4 hours.

5 Remove the parchment and cover with clarified butter (see Cook's Tip).

6 Garnish with a sprig of parsley and serve with slices of buttered brown bread.

COOK'S TIP

The Potted Smoked Chicken can be kept in the refrigerator for 2–3 days, but no longer as it does not contain any preservatives. It may be stored in the freezer for a maximum of 1 month.

COOK'S TIP

To make clarified butter: place 250 g/9 oz/1 cup butter in a saucepan and heat gently, skimming off the foam as the butter heats – the sediment will sink to the bottom of the pan. When the butter has completely melted, remove the pan from the heat and leave to stand for at least 4 minutes. Strain the butter through a piece of muslin (cheesecloth) into a bowl. Allow the butter to cool a little before spooning it over the surface of the potted chicken.

Cheesy Garlic Drummers

Ideal for informal parties, these tasty chicken drumsticks can be prepared for cooking a day in advance. Instead of baking the chicken drumsticks, you could cook them on the barbecue instead.

Serves 6

INGREDIENTS

15 g/¹/₂ oz/1 tbsp butter
1 garlic clove, crushed
3 tbsp chopped fresh parsley
125 g/4¹/₂ oz/¹/₂ cup
   ricotta cheese

4 tbsp grated Parmesan cheese
3 tbsp fresh breadcrumbs
12 chicken drumsticks
salt and pepper
lemon slices, to garnish

mixed salad leaves, to serve

1 Melt the butter in a pan. Add the garlic and fry gently, stirring, for 1 minute without browning.

2 Remove the pan from the heat and stir in the parsley, the cheeses, breadcrumbs and salt and pepper to taste.

3 Carefully loosen the skin around the chicken drumsticks.

4 Using a teaspoon, push about 1 tablespoon of the stuffing under the skin of each drumstick. Arrange the drumsticks in a large baking tin (pan).

5 Bake in a preheated oven, 190°C/375°F/ Gas Mark 5, for about 45 minutes. Serve hot or cold, garnished with lemon slices.

COOK'S TIP

Any strongly flavoured cheese can be used instead of the Parmesan. Try a mature Cheddar or use another Italian cheese, such as pecorino.

COOK'S TIP

Freshly grated Parmesan has more 'bite' than ready-packed grated Parmesan from supermarkets. Grate only as much as you need and wrap the rest up in foil – it will then keep for several months in the refrigerator.

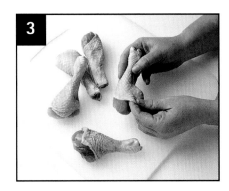

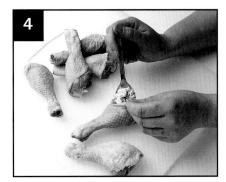

Chicken Rarebit

A tasty dish that can be served alone as a snack or to accompany a light, clear soup.

Serves 4

INGREDIENTS

250 g/9 oz/2 cups grated
   Wensleydale cheese
250 g/9 oz/1⅓ cups shredded,
   cooked chicken
1 tbsp butter
1 tbsp Worcestershire sauce

1 tsp dry English mustard
2 tsp plain (all-purpose) flour
4 tbsp mild beer
4 slices of bread
salt and pepper

1 tbsp chopped fresh parsley, to
   garnish
cherry tomatoes, to serve

1 Place the grated Wensleydale cheese, chicken, butter, Worcestershire sauce, mustard, plain (all-purpose) flour and beer in a small saucepan. Mix all the ingredients together then season with salt and pepper to taste.

2 Gently bring the mixture to the boil then remove from the heat immediately.

3 Using a wooden spoon, beat until the mixture becomes creamy in texture. Allow the mixture to cool.

4 Once the chicken mixture has cooled, toast the bread on both sides and spread with the chicken mixture.

5 Place under a hot grill (broiler) until bubbling and golden brown.

6 Sprinkle with a little chopped parsley and serve with cherry tomatoes.

COOK'S TIP

This is a variation of Welsh rarebit which does not traditionally contain chicken. Welsh rarebit topped with a poached egg is called buck rarebit.

Waldorf Summer Chicken Salad

This colourful and healthy dish is a variation of a classic salad. Served with crusty brown rolls, it is an ideal light meal for a summer's day

Serves 4

INGREDIENTS

500 g/1 lb 2 oz red apples, diced
3 tbsp fresh lemon juice
150 ml/¹/₄ pint/²/₃ cup light
   mayonnaise
1 head of celery
4 shallots, sliced

1 garlic clove, crushed
90 g/3 oz/³/₄ cup walnuts, chopped
500 g/1 lb 2 oz cooked chicken,
   cubed
1 Cos lettuce

pepper
sliced apple and walnuts, to garnish

1 Place the apples in a bowl with the lemon juice and 1 tablespoon of mayonnaise. Leave for 40 minutes.

2 Using a sharp knife, slice the celery very thinly.

3 Add the celery, shallots, garlic and walnuts to the apple and mix together.

4 Stir in the remaining mayonnaise and blend thoroughly.

5 Add the cooked chicken to the bowl and mix well.

6 Line a glass salad bowl or serving dish with the lettuce leaves. Pile the chicken salad into the centre, sprinkle with pepper and garnish with the apple slices and walnuts.

COOK'S TIP

Soaking the apples in lemon juice prevents discoloration.

COOK'S TIP

Instead of the shallots, use spring onions (scallions) for a milder flavour. Trim the spring onions (scallions) and slice finely.

Old English Spicy Chicken Salad

For this simple, refreshing summer salad you can use leftover roast chicken, or ready-roasted chicken to save time. Add the dressing just before serving, or the spinach will lose its crispness.

Serves 4

INGREDIENTS

250 g/9 oz young spinach leaves
3 sticks (stalks) celery, sliced thinly
1/2 cucumber
2 spring onions (scallions)
3 tbsp chopped fresh parsley
350g/12 oz boneless,
    roast chicken, sliced thinly

DRESSING:
2.5 cm/1 inch piece fresh ginger
    root, grated finely
3 tbsp olive oil
1 tbsp white wine vinegar
1 tbsp clear honey
1/2 tsp ground cinnamon
salt and pepper

smoked almonds, to garnish
(optional)

1 Thoroughly wash the spinach leaves, then pat dry with paper towels.

2 Using a sharp knife, thinly slice the celery, cucumber and spring onions (scallions). Toss in a large bowl with the spinach leaves and parsley.

3 Transfer to serving plates and arrange the chicken on top of the salad.

4 In a screw-topped jar, combine all the dressing ingredients and shake well to mix. Season the dressing with salt and pepper to taste, then pour over the salad. Sprinkle with a few smoked almonds, if using.

VARIATION

Substitute lamb's lettuce (corn salad) for the spinach, if you prefer.

VARIATION

Fresh young spinach leaves go particularly well with fruit – try adding a few fresh raspberries or nectarine slices to make an even more refreshing salad.

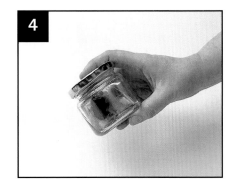

Suprême of Chicken with Pear & Blue Cheese Salad

The sweetness of the pears complements perfectly the sharp taste of the blue cheese in this delicious warm salad.

Serves 6

INGREDIENTS

50 ml/2 fl oz/$\frac{1}{4}$ cup olive oil
6 shallots, sliced
1 garlic clove, crushed
2 tbsp chopped fresh tarragon
1 tbsp English mustard
6 skinless, boneless chicken breasts
1 tbsp flour
150 ml/$\frac{1}{4}$ pint/$\frac{2}{3}$ cup chicken stock

1 apple, diced finely
1 tbsp chopped walnuts
2 tbsp double (heavy) cream
salt and pepper

SALAD:
250 g/9 oz/$3\frac{1}{2}$ cups cooked rice
2 large pears, diced

150 g/5$\frac{1}{2}$ oz/1 cup blue cheese, diced
1 red (bell) pepper, diced
1 tbsp chopped fresh coriander (cilantro)
1 tbsp sesame oil

1 Place the olive oil, shallots, garlic, tarragon and mustard in a deep bowl. Season well and mix the ingredients together thoroughly.

2 Place the chicken in the marinade to coat completely, cover with cling film (plastic wrap) and chill in the refrigerator for about 4 hours.

3 Drain the chicken, reserving the marinade. Quickly fry the chicken in a large, deep non-stick frying pan (skillet) for 4 minutes on both sides. Transfer the chicken to a warm serving dish.

4 Add the marinade to the pan, bring to the boil and sprinkle with the flour. Add the chicken stock, apple and walnuts and

gently simmer for 5 minutes. Return the chicken to the sauce, add the double (heavy) cream and cook for 2 minutes.

5 Mix the salad ingredients together, place a little on each plate and top with a chicken breast and a spoonful of the sauce.

Quick Dishes

One of the marvellous qualities of chicken is that when cut into small pieces, it can be cooked very quickly, which is welcome for those of us who are too busy to spend a lot of time preparing meals. In this section, you can select a tasty nutritious dish that won't take hours to make. Pasta makes a perfect partner for chicken as it is also quick to cook – Italian Chicken Spirals look impressive and will fool guests into thinking that you have spent hours slaving away in the kitchen. Chicken breasts are cooked with a delicious basil, hazelnut and garlic filling and then served on a bed of pasta, olives and sun-dried tomatoes. Smaller cuts of chicken are also ideal for stir-fries that can be quickly cooked to produce tender, moist and flavourful chicken. Speedy Peanut Pan-fry is a crunchy stir-fry that is served with noodles. Risottos are also an excellent choice for when you are in a hurry – this chapter contains two risotto recipes although the variations for risotto are endless!

Harlequin Chicken

This colourful, simple dish will tempt the appetites of all the family – it is ideal for toddlers, who enjoy the fun shapes of the multi-coloured (bell) peppers.

Serves 4

INGREDIENTS

10 skinless, boneless chicken thighs
1 medium onion
1 each medium red, green
   and yellow (bell) peppers
1 tbsp sunflower oil

400 g/14 oz can chopped
   tomatoes
2 tbsp chopped fresh parsley
pepper

wholemeal (whole wheat) bread and
   a green salad, to serve

1 Using a sharp knife, cut the chicken thighs into bite-sized pieces.

2 Peel and thinly slice the onion. Halve and deseed the (bell) peppers and cut into small diamond shapes.

3 Heat the oil in a shallow frying pan (skillet). Add the chicken and onion and fry quickly until golden.

4 Add the (bell) peppers, cook for 2–3 minutes, then stir in the tomatoes and parsley and season with pepper.

5 Cover tightly and simmer for about 15 minutes, until the chicken and vegetables are tender. Serve hot with wholemeal (whole wheat) bread and a green salad.

COOK'S TIP

You can use dried parsley instead of fresh but remember that you only need about one half of dried to fresh.

COOK'S TIP

If you are making this dish for small children, the chicken can be finely chopped or minced (ground) first.

Steamed Chicken & Spring Vegetable Parcels

A healthy recipe with a delicate oriental flavour, ideal for tender young summer vegetables. You'll need large spinach leaves to wrap around the chicken, but make sure they are young leaves.

Serves 4

INGREDIENTS

4 boneless, skinless
  chicken breasts
1 tsp ground lemon grass
2 spring onions (scallions),
  chopped finely
250 g/9 oz/1 cup young carrots

250 g/9 oz/1³/₄ cups young
  courgettes (zucchini)
2 sticks (stalks) celery
1 tsp light soy sauce
250 g/9 oz/³/₄ cup spinach leaves
2 tsp sesame oil

salt and pepper

1 With a sharp knife, make a slit through one side of each chicken breast, to open out a large pocket. Sprinkle the inside of the pocket with lemon grass, salt and pepper. Tuck the spring onions (scallions) into the pockets.

2 Trim the carrots, courgettes and celery then cut into small matchsticks. Plunge them into a pan of boiling water for 1 minute, drain and toss in the soy sauce.

3 Pack the vegetables into the pockets in each chicken breast and fold over firmly to enclose. Reserve any remaining vegetables. Wash the spinach leaves thoroughly, then drain and pat dry with paper towels. Wrap the chicken breasts firmly in the spinach leaves to enclose completely. If the leaves are too firm to wrap the chicken easily, steam them for a few seconds until they are softened and flexible.

4 Place the wrapped chicken in a steamer and steam over rapidly boiling water for 20–25 minutes, depending on size.

5 Stir-fry any leftover vegetable sticks and spinach for 1–2 minutes in the sesame oil and serve with the chicken.

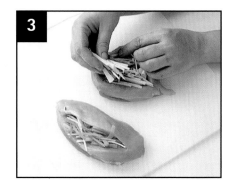

Chicken with Two (Bell) Pepper Sauce

*This quick and simple dish is colourful and healthy.
It would be perfect for an impromptu lunch or supper dish.*

Serves 4

INGREDIENTS

2 tbsp olive oil
2 medium onions, chopped finely
2 garlic cloves, crushed
2 red (bell) peppers, chopped
good pinch cayenne pepper
2 tsp tomato purée (paste)

2 yellow (bell) peppers, chopped
pinch of dried basil
4 skinless, boneless
  chicken breasts
150 ml/^{1}/4 pint/^{2}/3 cup
  dry white wine

150 ml/^{1}/4 pint/^{2}/3 cup
  chicken stock
bouquet garni
salt and pepper
fresh herbs, to garnish

1 Heat 1 tablespoon of oil in each of two medium-sized saucepans. Place half the chopped onions, 1 of the garlic cloves, the red (bell) peppers, the cayenne pepper and the tomato purée (paste) in one of the saucepans. Place the remaining onion, garlic, yellow (bell) peppers and basil in the other pan.

2 Cover each pan and cook over a very low heat for 1 hour until the (bell) peppers are soft. If either mixture becomes dry, add a little water. Work each mixture separately in a food processor, then sieve separately.

3 Return the separate mixtures to the pans and season. The two sauces can be gently re-heated while the chicken is cooking.

4 Put the chicken breasts into a frying pan (skillet) and add the wine and stock. Add the bouquet garni and bring the liquid to simmer. Cook the chicken for about 20 minutes until tender.

5 To serve, pour a serving of each sauce on to four serving plates, slice the chicken breasts and arrange on the plates. Garnish with fresh herbs.

COOK'S TIP

Make your own bouquet garni by tying together sprigs of your favourite herbs with string, or wrap up dried herbs in a piece of muslin. A popular combination is thyme, parsley and bay.

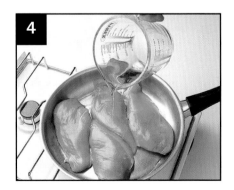

Chicken Risotto à la Milanese

This famous dish is known throughout the world, and it is perhaps the best known of all Italian risottos, although there are many variations.

Serves 4

INGREDIENTS

125 g/4^{1}/$_{2}$ oz/^{1}/$_{2}$ cup butter
900 g/2 lb chicken meat, sliced thinly
1 large onion, chopped
500 g/1 lb 2 oz/2^{1}/$_{2}$ cups risotto rice
600 ml/1 pint/2^{1}/$_{2}$ cups chicken stock

150 ml/^{1}/$_{2}$ pint/^{2}/$_{3}$ cup white wine
1 tsp crumbled saffron
salt and pepper
60 g/2 oz/^{1}/$_{2}$ cup grated
   Parmesan cheese, to serve

1 Heat 60 g/2 oz/4 tbsp of butter in a deep frying pan (skillet), and fry the chicken and onion until golden brown.

2 Add the rice, stir well, and cook for 15 minutes.

3 Heat the stock until boiling and gradually add to the rice. Add the white wine, saffron, salt and pepper to taste and mix well. Simmer gently for 20 minutes, stirring occasionally, and adding more stock if the risotto becomes too dry.

4 Leave to stand for a few minutes and just before serving add a little more stock and simmer for a further 10 minutes. Serve the risotto, sprinkled with the grated Parmesan cheese and the remaining butter.

COOK'S TIP

A risotto should have moist but separate grains. Stock should be added a little at a time and only when the last addition has been completely absorbed.

VARIATION

The possibilities for risotto are endless – try adding the following just at the end of cooking time: cashew nuts and sweetcorn, lightly sautéed courgettes (zucchini) and basil, or artichokes and oyster mushrooms.

Elizabethan Chicken

*Chicken is surprisingly delicious when combined
with fruits such as grapes or gooseberries.*

Serves 4

INGREDIENTS

15 g/¹/₂ oz/1 tbsp butter
1 tbsp sunflower oil
4 skinless, boneless
   chicken breasts
4 shallots, finely chopped
150 ml/¹/₂ pint/²/₃ cup
   chicken stock

1 tbsp cider vinegar
175 g/6 oz/1 cup halved
   seedless grapes
120 ml/4 floz/¹/₂ cup
   double (heavy) cream
1 tsp freshly grated nutmeg

cornflour (cornstarch), to thicken,
   (optional)
salt and pepper

1 Heat the butter and
sunflower oil in a wide,
flameproof casserole or pan and
quickly fry the chicken breasts
until golden brown, turning once.
Remove the chicken breasts and
keep warm while you are cooking
the shallots.

2 Add the chopped shallots to
the pan and fry gently until
softened and lightly browned.
Return the chicken breasts to
the pan.

3 Add the chicken stock and
cider vinegar to the pan, bring
to the boil then cover and simmer
gently for 10–12 minutes, stirring
occasionally.

4 Transfer the chicken to a
serving dish. Add the grapes,
cream and nutmeg to the pan.
Heat through, seasoning with salt
and pepper to taste. Add a little
cornflour (cornstarch) to thicken
the sauce, if desired. Pour the
sauce over the chicken and serve.

VARIATION

*If desired, add a little dry white
wine or vermouth to the sauce
in step 3.*

Speedy Peanut Pan-fry

A complete main course cooked within ten minutes. Thread egg noodles are the ideal accompaniment because they can be cooked quickly and easily while the stir-fry sizzles.

Serves 4

INGREDIENTS

300 g/10^1/2 oz/2 cups courgettes (zucchini)
250 g/9 oz/1^1/3 cups baby corn (corn-on-the-cob)
300 g/10^1/2 oz/3^3/4 cups button mushrooms
250 g/9 oz/3 cups thread egg noodles

2 tbsp corn oil
1 tbsp sesame oil
8 boneless chicken thighs or 4 breasts, sliced thinly
350 g/12 oz/1^1/2 cups bean sprouts
4 tbsp smooth peanut butter
2 tbsp soy sauce
2 tbsp lime or lemon juice

60 g/2 oz/^{1}/2 cup roasted peanuts
pepper
coriander (cilantro), to garnish

1 Using a sharp knife, trim and thinly slice the courgettes (zucchini), corn (corn-on-the-cob) and button mushrooms.

2 Bring a large pan of lightly salted boiling water to the boil and cook the noodles for 3–4 minutes. Meanwhile, heat the corn oil and sesame oil in a large frying pan (skillet) or wok and fry the chicken over a fairly high heat for 1 minute.

3 Add the sliced courgettes (zucchini), corn (corn-on-the-cob) and button mushrooms and stir-fry for 5 minutes.

4 Add the bean sprouts, peanut butter, soy sauce, lime or lemon juice and pepper, then cook for a further 2 minutes.

5 Drain the noodles, transfer to a serving dish and scatter with the peanuts. Serve with the stir-fried chicken and vegetables, garnished with a sprig of fresh coriander (cilantro).

COOK'S TIP

Try serving this stir-fry with rice sticks. These are broad, pale, translucent ribbon noodles made from ground rice.

Parma-wrapped Chicken Cushions

*Stuffed with creamy ricotta, nutmeg and spinach, then wrapped with wafer thin
slices of Parma ham (prosciutto) and gently cooked in white wine.*

Serves 4

INGREDIENTS

125 g/4^1/2 oz/^{1}/2 cup frozen spinach,
  defrosted
125 g/4^1/2 oz/^{1}/2 cup ricotta cheese
pinch grated nutmeg
4 skinless, boneless chicken breasts,
  each weighing 175 g/6 oz

4 Parma ham (prosciutto) slices
25 g/1 oz/2 tbsp butter
1 tbsp olive oil
12 small onions or shallots
125 g/4^1/2 oz/1^1/2 cups button
  mushrooms, sliced

1 tbsp plain (all-purpose) flour
150 ml/^{1}/4 pint/^{2}/3 cup dry white
  or red wine
300 ml/^{1}/2 pint/1^1/4 cups
  chicken stock
salt and pepper

1 Put the spinach into a sieve (strainer) and press out the water with a spoon. Mix with the ricotta and nutmeg and season with salt and pepper to taste.

2 Using a sharp knife, slit each chicken breast through the side and enlarge each cut to form a pocket. Fill with the spinach mixture, reshape the chicken breasts, wrap each breast tightly in a slice of ham and secure with cocktail sticks. Cover and chill in the refrigerator.

3 Heat the butter and oil in a frying pan (skillet) and brown the chicken breasts for 2 minutes on each side. Transfer the chicken to a large, shallow ovenproof dish and keep warm until required.

4 Fry the onions and mushrooms for 2–3 minutes until lightly browned. Stir in the plain (all-purpose) flour then gradually add the wine and stock. Bring to the boil, stirring constantly. Season and spoon the mixture around the chicken.

5 Cook the chicken uncovered in a preheated oven, 200°C/400°F/Gas Mark 6, for 20 minutes. Turn the breasts over and cook for a further 10 minutes. Remove the cocktail sticks and serve with the sauce, together with carrot purée and green beans, if wished.

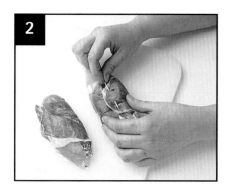

Poached Breast of Chicken with Whisky Sauce

After cooking with stock and vegetables, chicken breasts are served with a velvety sauce made from whisky and crème fraîche.

Serves 6

INGREDIENTS

25 g/1 oz/2 tbsp butter
60 g/2 oz/^{1}/$_2$ cup shredded leeks
60 g/2 oz/^{1}/$_3$ cup diced carrot
60 g/2 oz/^{1}/$_4$ cup diced celery
4 shallots, sliced

600 ml/1 pint/2^1/$_2$ cups chicken stock
6 chicken breasts
50 ml/2 fl oz/^{1}/$_4$ cup whisky
200 ml/7 fl oz/1 scant cup crème fraîche

2 tbsp freshly grated horseradish
1 tsp honey, warmed
1 tsp chopped fresh parsley
salt and pepper
sprig of fresh parsley, to garnish

1 Melt the butter in a large saucepan and add the leeks, carrot, celery and shallots. Cook for 3 minutes, add half the chicken stock and cook for about 8 minutes.

2 Add the remaining chicken stock, bring to the boil, add the chicken breasts and cook for 10 minutes.

3 Remove the chicken and thinly slice. Place on a large, hot serving dish and keep warm until required.

4 In another saucepan, heat the whisky until reduced by half. Strain the chicken stock through a fine sieve, add to the pan and reduce the liquid by half.

5 Add the crème fraîche, the horseradish and the honey. Heat gently and add the chopped parsley and salt and pepper to taste. Stir until well blended.

6 Pour a little of the whisky sauce around the chicken and pour the remaining sauce into a sauceboat to serve.

7 Serve with a vegetable patty made from the leftover vegetables, mashed potato and fresh vegetables. Garnish with the parsley sprig.

Devilled Chicken

Chicken is spiked with cayenne pepper and paprika and finished off with a fruity sauce.

Serves 2-3

INGREDIENTS

25 g/1 oz/^{1}/$_4$ cup plain (all-purpose)
   flour
1 tbsp cayenne pepper
1 tsp paprika
350 g/12 oz skinless,
   boneless chicken, diced

25 g/1 oz/2 tbsp butter
1 onion, chopped finely
450 ml/16 fl oz/1^7/$_8$ cups milk,
   warmed
4 tbsp apple purée

125 g/4^1/$_2$ oz/^{3}/$_4$ cup green (white)
   grapes
150 ml/^{1}/$_4$ pint/^{2}/$_3$ cup soured cream
sprinkle of paprika

1 Mix the flour, cayenne pepper and paprika together and use to coat the chicken.

2 Shake off any excess flour. Melt the butter in a saucepan and gently fry the chicken with the onion for 4 minutes.

3 Stir in the flour and spice mixture. Add the milk slowly, stirring until the sauce thickens.

4 Simmer until the sauce is smooth.

5 Add the apple purée and grapes and simmer gently for 20 minutes.

6 Transfer the chicken and devilled sauce to a serving dish and top with soured cream and a sprinkle of paprika.

VARIATION

For a healthier alternative to soured cream, use natural (unsweetened) yogurt.

COOK'S TIP

Add more paprika if desired – as it is quite a mild spice, you can add plenty without it being too overpowering.

Italian Chicken Spirals

Steaming allows you to cook without fat, and these little foil parcels retain all the natural juices of the chicken while cooking conveniently over the pasta while it boils.

Serves 4

INGREDIENTS

4 skinless, boneless, chicken breasts
25 g/1 oz/1 cup fresh basil leaves
15 g/¹/₂ oz/2 tbsp hazelnuts
1 garlic clove, crushed
250 g/9 oz/2 cups wholemeal
  (whole wheat) pasta spirals

2 sun-dried tomatoes
  or fresh tomatoes
1 tbsp lemon juice
1 tbsp olive oil
1 tbsp capers
60 g/2 oz/¹/₂ cup black olives

salt and pepper

1 Beat the chicken breasts with a rolling pin to flatten evenly.

2 Place the basil and hazelnuts in a food processor and process until finely chopped. Mix with the garlic, salt and pepper.

3 Spread the basil mixture over the chicken breasts and roll up from one short end to enclose the filling. Wrap the chicken roll tightly in foil so that they hold their shape, then seal the ends well.

4 Bring a large pan of lightly salted water to the boil and cook the pasta until tender, but still firm to the bite.

5 Place the chicken parcels in a steamer basket or colander set over the pan, cover tightly, and steam for 10 minutes. Meanwhile, dice the tomatoes.

6 Drain the pasta and return to the pan with the lemon juice, olive oil, tomatoes, capers and olives. Heat through.

7 Pierce the chicken with a skewer to make sure that the juices run clear and not pink, then slice the chicken, arrange over the pasta and serve.

VARIATION

Sun-dried tomatoes have a wonderful, rich flavour, but if you can't find them use fresh tomatoes.

Garlicky Chicken Cushions

Stuffed with creamy ricotta, spinach and garlic, then gently cooked in a rich tomato sauce, this is a suitable dish to make ahead of time.

Serves 4

INGREDIENTS

4 part-boned chicken breasts
125 g/4$^{1}/_{2}$ oz/$^{1}/_{2}$ cup frozen
   spinach, defrosted
150 g/5$^{1}/_{2}$ oz/$^{1}/_{2}$ cup ricotta cheese
2 garlic cloves, crushed
1 tbsp olive oil

1 onion, chopped
1 red (bell) pepper, sliced
400 g/14 oz can chopped tomatoes
6 tbsp wine or chicken stock
10 stuffed olives, sliced

salt and pepper
pasta, to serve

1 Make a slit between the skin and meat on one side of each chicken breast. Lift the skin to form a pocket, being careful to leave the skin attached to the other side.

2 Put the spinach into a sieve and press out the water with a spoon. Mix with the ricotta, half the garlic and seasoning.

3 Spoon the spinach mixture under the skin of each chicken breast then secure the edge of the skin with cocktail sticks.

4 Heat the oil in a frying pan (skillet), add the onion and fry for a minute, stirring. Add the remaining garlic and red (bell) pepper and cook for 2 minutes. Stir in the tomatoes, wine or stock, olives and seasoning. Set the sauce aside and chill the chicken if preparing in advance.

5 Bring the sauce to the boil, pour into a shallow ovenproof dish and arrange the chicken breasts on top in a single layer.

6 Cook, uncovered in a preheated oven, 200°C/400°F/ Gas Mark 6, for 35 minutes until the chicken is golden and cooked through. Test by making a slit in one of the chicken breasts with a skewer to make sure the juices run clear and not pink. Spoon a little of the sauce over the chicken breasts then transfer to serving plates. Serve with pasta.

Chicken Strips & Dips

Very simple to make and easy to eat with fingers, this dish can be served warm for a light lunch or cold as part of a buffet.

Serves 2

INGREDIENTS

2 boneless chicken breasts
15 g/¹⁄₂ oz/2 tbsp plain (all-purpose) flour
1 tbsp sunflower oil

PEANUT DIP:
3 tbsp smooth or crunchy peanut butter
4 tbsp natural (unsweetened) yogurt
1 tsp grated orange rind
orange juice (optional)

TOMATO DIP:
5 tbsp creamy fromage frais
1 medium tomato
2 tsp tomato purée (paste)
1 tsp chopped fresh chives

1 Using a sharp knife, slice the chicken into fairly thin strips and toss in the flour to coat.

2 Heat the oil in a non-stick pan and fry the chicken until golden and thoroughly cooked. Remove the chicken strips from the pan and drain well on absorbent paper towels.

3 To make the peanut dip, mix together all the ingredients in a bowl (if liked, add a little orange juice to thin the consistency).

4 To make the tomato dip, chop the tomato and mix with the remaining ingredients.

5 Serve the chicken strips with the dips and a selection of vegetable sticks for dipping.

VARIATION

For a lower-fat alternative, poach the strips of chicken in a small amount of boiling chicken stock for 6–8 minutes.

VARIATION

For a refreshing guacamole dip, combine 1 mashed avocado, 2 finely chopped spring onions (scallions), 1 chopped tomato, 1 crushed garlic clove and a squeeze of lemon juice. Remember to add the lemon juice immediately after the avocado has been mashed to prevent discoloration.

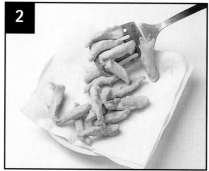

Chicken Lady Jayne

If you prefer, just use boneless chicken breasts in this recipe.
This dish has a surprising combination of coffee and brandy flavours.

Serves 4

INGREDIENTS

4 chicken breasts or suprêmes, each
about 125 g/4^1/$_2$ oz
4 tbsp corn oil
8 shallots, sliced
rind and juice of 1 lemon

2 tsp Worcestershire sauce
4 tbsp chicken stock
1 tbsp chopped fresh parsley
3 tbsp coffee liqueur
3 tbsp brandy, warmed

1 Place the chicken breasts or suprêmes on a chopping board, cover with cling film (plastic wrap) and pound them until flattened with a wooden meat mallet or a rolling pin.

2 Heat the oil in a large frying pan (skillet) and fry the chicken for 3 minutes on each side. Add the shallots and cook for a further 3 minutes.

3 Sprinkle with lemon juice and lemon rind and add the Worcestershire sauce and chicken stock. Cook for 2 minutes, then sprinkle with the chopped fresh parsley.

4 Add the coffee liqueur and the brandy and flame the chicken by lighting the spirit with a taper or long match. Cook until the flame is extinguished and serve.

COOK'S TIP

Flattening the suprêmes means that they take less time to cook.

COOK'S TIP

A suprême is a chicken fillet that sometimes has part of the wing bone remaining. Chicken breasts can be used instead.

Golden Glazed Chicken

A glossy glaze with sweet and fruity flavours coats chicken breasts in this tasty recipe.

Serves 6

INGREDIENTS

6 boneless chicken breasts
1 tsp turmeric
1 tbsp wholegrain
    (whole-grain) mustard
300 ml/$\frac{1}{2}$ pint/$1\frac{1}{4}$ cups
    orange juice

2 tbsp clear honey
2 tbsp sunflower oil
350 g/12 oz/$1\frac{1}{2}$ cups
    long grain rice
1 orange
3 tbsp chopped mint

salt and pepper
mint sprigs, to garnish

1 With a sharp knife, mark the surface of the chicken breasts in a diamond pattern. Mix together the turmeric, mustard, orange juice and honey and pour over the chicken. Chill until required.

2 Lift the chicken from the marinade and pat dry on paper towels.

3 Heat the oil in a wide pan, add the chicken and sauté until golden, turning once. Drain off any excess oil. Pour over the marinade, cover and simmer for 10–15 minutes until the chicken is tender.

4 Boil the rice in lightly salted water until tender and drain well. Finely grate the rind from the orange and stir into the rice with the mint.

5 Using a sharp knife, remove the peel and white pith from the orange and cut the flesh into segments.

6 Serve the chicken with the orange and mint rice, garnished with orange segments and mint sprigs.

VARIATION

To make a slightly sharper sauce, use small grapefruit instead of the oranges.

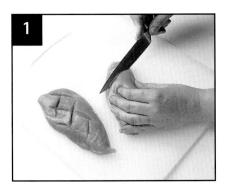

Mediterranean Chicken Parcels

This method of cooking makes the chicken aromatic and succulent. It also reduces the amount of oil needed since the chicken and vegetables cook in their own juices.

Serves 6

INGREDIENTS

1 tbsp olive oil
6 skinless chicken breast fillets
250 g/9 oz/2 cups Mozzarella
  cheese

500 g/1 lb 2 oz/3^1/$_2$ cups courgettes
  (zucchini), sliced
6 large tomatoes, sliced
1 small bunch fresh basil or oregano

pepper
rice or pasta, to serve

1 Cut six pieces of foil each about 25cm/10 inches square. Brush the foil squares lightly with oil and set aside until required.

2 With a sharp knife, slash each chicken breast at intervals, then slice the Mozzarella cheese and place between the cuts in the chicken.

3 Divide the courgettes (zucchini) and tomatoes between the pieces of foil and sprinkle with black pepper. Tear or roughly chop the basil or oregano and scatter over the vegetables in each parcel.

4 Place the chicken on top of each pile of vegetables then wrap in the foil to enclose the chicken and vegetables, tucking in the ends.

5 Place on a baking tray (cookie sheet) and bake in a preheated oven, 200°C/400°C/Gas Mark 6, for about 30 minutes.

6 To serve, unwrap each foil parcel and serve with rice or pasta.

COOK'S TIP

To aid cooking, place the vegetables and chicken on the shiny side of the foil so that once the parcel is wrapped up the dull surface of the foil is facing outwards. This ensures that the heat is absorbed into the parcel and not reflected away from it.

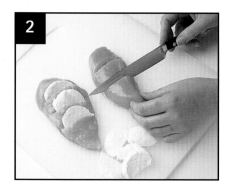
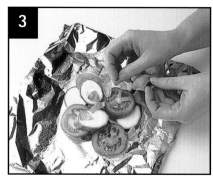
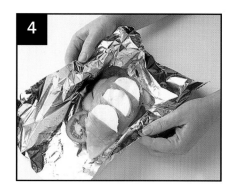

Chicken, Corn & Mangetout (Snow Pea) Sauté

This quick and healthy dish is stir-fried, which means you need use only the minimum of fat. If you don't have a wok, use a wide frying pan (skillet) instead.

Serves 4

INGREDIENTS

4 skinless, boneless
  chicken breasts
250 g/9 oz/1¹⁄₃ cups baby sweetcorn
  (corn-on-the-cob)
250 g/9 oz mangetout
  (snow peas)

2 tbsp sunflower oil
1 tbsp sherry vinegar
1 tbsp honey
1 tbsp light soy sauce

1 tbsp sunflower seeds
pepper
rice or egg noodles, to serve

1 Using a sharp knife, slice the chicken breasts into long, thin strips. Cut the baby sweetcorn (corn-on-the-cob) in half lengthways and top and tail the mangetout (snow peas). Set the vegetables aside until required.

2 Heat the sunflower oil in a wok or a wide frying pan (skillet) and fry the chicken over a fairly high heat, stirring constantly, for 1 minute.

3 Add the corn and mangetout (snow peas) and stir over a moderate heat for 5–8 minutes, until evenly cooked.

4 Mix together the sherry vinegar, honey and soy sauce and stir into the pan with the sunflower seeds. Season with pepper to taste. Cook, stirring constantly, for 1 minute. Serve the sauté hot with rice or Chinese egg noodles.

COOK'S TIP

Rice vinegar or balsamic vinegar makes a good substitute for the sherry vinegar.

Savoury Chicken Sausages

Served with a smooth creamy tomato sauce,
this makes an excellent light lunch with freshly baked cheese bread.

Serves 4–6

INGREDIENTS

175 g/6 oz/3 cups fresh breadcrumbs
250 g/9 oz cooked chicken, minced
   (ground)
1 small leek, chopped finely
pinch each of mixed herbs and
   mustard powder

2 eggs, separated
4 tbsp milk
crisp breadcrumbs for coating
25 g/1 oz/2 tbsp beef dripping(s)
salt and pepper

1 In a large clean bowl, combine the breadcrumbs, minced (ground) chicken, leek, mixed herbs and mustard powder, and season with salt and pepper. Mix together until thoroughly incorporated.

2 Add 1 whole egg and an egg yolk with a little milk to bind the mixture.

3 Divide the mixture into 6 or 8 and shape into thick or thin sausages.

4 Whisk the remaining egg white until frothy. Coat the sausages first in the egg white and then in the crisp breadcrumbs.

5 Heat the dripping(s) and fry the sausages for 6 minutes until golden brown. Serve.

COOK'S TIP

Make your own minced (ground)
chicken by working lean cuts of
chicken in a food processor.

VARIATION

If you want to lower the saturated
fat content of this recipe, use a little
oil for frying instead of
the dripping(s).

Golden Chicken Risotto

If you prefer, ordinary long grain rice can be used instead of risotto rice, but it won't give you the traditional, deliciously creamy texture that is typical of Italian risottos.

Serves 4

INGREDIENTS

2 tbsp sunflower oil
15 g/^{1}/$_2$ oz/1 tbsp butter
  or margarine
1 medium leek, thinly sliced
1 large yellow (bell) pepper, diced
3 skinless, boneless chicken breasts,
  diced
350 g/12 oz round grain
  (arborio) rice

few strands saffron
1.5 litres/2^3/$_4$ pints/6^1/$_4$ cups chicken
  stock
200 g/7 oz can sweetcorn
  (corn-on-the-cob)
60 g/2 oz/^{1}/$_2$ cup toasted
  unsalted peanuts

60 g/2 oz/^{1}/$_2$ cup grated
  Parmesan cheese
salt and pepper

1 Heat the oil and butter or margarine in a large saucepan. Fry the leek and (bell) pepper for 1 minute then stir in the chicken and cook, stirring until golden brown.

2 Stir in the rice and cook for 2–3 minutes.

3 Stir in the saffron strands, and salt and pepper to taste.

Add the stock, a little at a time, cover and cook over a low heat, stirring occasionally, for about 20 minutes, until the rice is tender and most of the liquid is absorbed. Do not let the risotto dry out – add more stock if necessary.

4 Stir in the sweetcorn (corn-on-the-cob), peanuts and Parmesan cheese, then adjust the seasoning to taste. Serve hot.

COOK'S TIP

Risottos can be frozen, before adding the Parmesan cheese, for up to 1 month, but remember to reheat this risotto thoroughly as it contains chicken.

Quick Chicken Bake

This recipe is a type of cottage pie and is just as versatile. Add vegetables and herbs of your choice, depending on what you have at hand.

Serves 4

INGREDIENTS

500 g/1 lb 2 oz minced (ground) chicken
1 large onion, chopped finely
2 carrots, diced finely
25 g/1 oz/2 tbsp plain (all-purpose) flour
1 tbsp tomato purée (paste)

300 ml/1¹/₂ pint/1¹/₄ cups chicken stock
pinch of fresh thyme
900 g/2 lb potatoes, creamed with butter and milk and highly seasoned
90 g/3 oz/³/₄ cup grated Lancashire cheese

salt and pepper
peas, to serve

1 Dry-fry the minced (ground) chicken, onion and carrots in a non-stick saucepan for 5 minutes, stirring frequently.

2 Sprinkle the chicken with the flour and simmer for a further 2 minutes.

3 Gradually blend in the tomato purée (paste) and stock then simmer for 15 minutes. Season and add the thyme.

4 Transfer the chicken and vegetable mixture to an ovenproof casserole and allow to cool.

5 Spoon the mashed potato over the chicken mixture and sprinkle with the Lancashire cheese. Bake in a preheated oven, 200°C/400°F/Gas Mark 6, for 20 minutes, or until the cheese is bubbling and golden, then serve with the peas.

VARIATION

Instead of Lancashire cheese, you could sprinkle Cotswold cheese over the top. This is a tasty blend of Double Gloucester, onion and chives, and is ideal for melting as a topping. Alternatively, you could use a mixture of cheeses, depending on whatever you have at hand.

Tom's Toad in the Hole

This unusual recipe uses chicken and Cumberland sausage,
which is then made into individual bite-sized cakes.

Serves 4–6

INGREDIENTS

125 g/4$^1\!/_2$ oz/1 cup plain
(all-purpose) flour
pinch of salt

1 egg, beaten
200 ml/7 fl oz/1 scant cup milk
75 ml/3 fl oz/$^1\!/_3$ cup water

2 tbsp beef dripping(s)
250 g/9 oz chicken breasts
250 g/9 oz Cumberland sausage

1 Mix the flour and salt in a bowl, make a well in the centre and add the beaten egg.

2 Add half the milk, and using a wooden spoon, work in the flour slowly.

3 Beat the mixture until smooth, then add the remaining milk and water.

4 Beat again until the mixture is smooth. Let the mixture stand for at least 1 hour.

5 Add the dripping(s) to individual baking tins (pans)

or to one large baking tin (pan). Cut up the chicken and sausage so that you get a generous piece in each individual tin (pan) or several scattered around the large tin (pan).

6 Heat in a preheated oven, 220°C/425°F/ Gas Mark 7, for 5 minutes until very hot. Remove the tins (pans) from the oven and pour in the batter, leaving space for the mixture to expand.

7 Return to the oven to cook for 35 minutes, until risen and golden brown. Do not open the oven door for at least 30 minutes.

8 Serve while hot, with chicken or onion gravy, or alone.

VARIATION

Use skinless, boneless chicken legs instead of chicken breast in the recipe. Cut up as directed. Instead of Cumberland sausage, use your favourite variety of sausage.

Casseroles & Roasts

Long, slow cooking means meltingly succulent meat with a good, rich flavour. Because chicken itself does not have a strong flavour, it marries happily with almost any other ingredient, herb or spice. The recipes in this section are drawn from many cuisines from around the world, and there are dishes from Italy, France, Hungary, the Caribbean, and from the USA. French classics include Bourguignonne of Chicken and Brittany Chicken Casserole.

The aroma of roasting chicken is always tempting and this section includes the traditional roast chicken, with all the trimmings, as well as many other imaginative treatments. Unusual stuffings to try are courgette (zucchini) and lime, marmalade, or oat and herb stuffing. Many of the recipes in this section exploit the complementary flavours of chicken and fruits and there are some enticing taste combinations including cranberries, black cherries, apples, peaches, oranges and mangoes.

Rustic Chicken & Orange Pot

*Low in fat and high in fibre, this colourful casserole
makes a healthy and hearty meal.*

Serves 4

INGREDIENTS

8 chicken drumsticks, skinned
1 tbsp wholemeal
    (whole wheat) flour
1 tbsp olive oil
2 medium red onions
1 garlic clove, crushed
1 tsp fennel seeds

1 bay leaf
finely grated rind and juice
    of 1 small orange
400 g/14 oz can chopped tomatoes
400 g/14 oz can cannellini
    or flageolet beans, drained
salt and black pepper

TOPPING:
3 thick slices wholemeal
    (whole wheat) bread
2 tsp olive oil

1 Toss the chicken drumsticks in the flour to coat evenly. Heat the oil in a non-stick or heavy saucepan and fry the chicken over a fairly high heat, turning frquently, until golden brown. Transfer to a large ovenproof casserole and keep warm until required.

2 Slice the red onions into thin wedges. Add to the pan and cook for a few minutes until lightly browned. Stir in the garlic.

3 Add the fennel seeds, bay leaf, orange rind and juice, tomatoes, beans and seasoning.

4 Cover tightly and cook in a preheated oven, 190°C/375°F/ Gas Mark 5, for 30–35 minutes until the chicken juices are clear and not pink when pierced through the thickest part with a metal skewer.

5 For the topping, cut the bread into small dice and toss in the

oil. Remove the lid from the casserole and top with the bread cubes. Bake for a further 15–20 minutes until the bread is golden and crisp. Serve hot.

COOK'S TIP

Choose beans which are canned in water with no added sugar or salt. Drain and rinse well before use.

Spiced Chicken Casserole

Spices, herbs, fruit, nuts and vegetables are combined to make an appealing casserole with lots of flavour.

Serves 4-6

INGREDIENTS

3 tbsp olive oil
900 g/2 lb chicken meat, sliced
10 shallots or pickling onions
3 carrots, chopped
60 g/2 oz/$^1/_2$ cup chestnuts, sliced
60 g/2 oz/$^1/_2$ cup flaked (slivered) almonds, toasted
1 tsp freshly grated nutmeg
3 tsp ground cinnamon

300 ml/$^1/_2$ pint/1$^1/_4$ cups white wine
300 ml/$^1/_2$ pint/1$^1/_4$ cups chicken stock
175 ml/6 fl oz/$^3/_4$ cup white wine vinegar
1 tbsp chopped fresh tarragon
1 tbsp chopped fresh flat leaf parsley
1 tbsp chopped fresh thyme
grated rind of 1 orange

1 tbsp dark muscovado sugar
125 g/4$^1/_2$ oz/$^3/_4$ cup seedless black grapes, halved
sea salt and pepper
fresh herbs, to garnish
wild rice or puréed potato, to serve

1 Heat the olive oil in a large saucepan and fry the chicken, shallots or pickling onions, and carrots for about 6 minutes or until browned.

2 Add the remaining ingredients, except the grapes, and simmer over a low heat for 2 hours until the meat is very tender. Stir the casserole occasionally.

3 Add the grapes just before serving and serve with wild rice or puréed potato. Garnish with herbs.

VARIATION

Experiment with different types of nuts and fruits – try sunflower seeds instead of the almonds, and add 2 fresh apricots, chopped.

COOK'S TIP

This casserole would also be delicious served with thick slices of crusty wholemeal (whole wheat) bread to soak up the sauce.

Country Chicken Hot-Pot

There are many regional versions of hot-pot, all using fresh, local ingredients Now, there are an endless variety of ingredients available all year, perfect for traditional one-pot cooking.

Serves 4

INGREDIENTS

4 chicken quarters
6 medium potatoes, cut
  into 5 mm/¼ inch slices
2 sprigs thyme
2 sprigs rosemary
2 bay leaves

200 g/7 oz/1 cup rindless, smoked
  streaky bacon, diced
1 large onion, chopped finely
200 g/7 oz/1 cup sliced carrots
150 ml/¼ pint/⅔ cup stout
25 g/1 oz/2 tbsp melted butter

salt and pepper

1 Remove the skin from the chicken quarters, if preferred.

2 Arrange a layer of potato slices in the bottom of a wide casserole. Season with salt and pepper, then add the thyme, rosemary and bay leaves.

3 Top with the chicken quarters, then sprinkle with the diced bacon, onion and carrots. Season well and arrange the remaining potato slices on top, overlapping slightly.

4 Pour over the stout, brush the potatoes with the melted butter and cover with a lid.

5 Bake in a preheated oven, 150°C/300°F/Gas Mark 2, for about 2 hours, uncovering for the last 30 minutes to allow the potatoes to brown. Serve hot.

COOK'S TIP

Serve the hot-pot with dumplings for a truly hearty meal.

VARIATION

This dish is also delicious with stewing lamb, cut into chunks. You can add different vegetables depending on what is in season – try leeks and swedes for a slightly sweeter flavour.

Fricassée of Chicken in Lime Sauce

The addition of lime juice and lime rind adds a delicious tangy flavour to this chicken stew.

Serves 4

INGREDIENTS

1 large chicken, cut into
   small portions
60 g/2 oz/$\frac{1}{2}$ cup flour, seasoned
2 tbsp oil
500 g/1 lb 2 oz baby onions
   or shallots, sliced

1 each green and red (bell) pepper,
   sliced thinly
150 ml/$\frac{1}{4}$ pint/$\frac{2}{3}$ cup chicken stock
juice and rind of 2 limes
2 chillies, chopped
2 tbsp oyster sauce

1 tsp Worcestershire sauce
salt and pepper

---

1 Coat the chicken pieces in the seasoned flour. Heat the oil in a large frying pan (skillet) and cook the chicken for about 4 minutes until browned all over.

2 Using a slotted spoon, transfer the chicken to a large, deep casserole and sprinkle with the sliced onions. Keep warm until required.

3 Slowly fry the (bell) peppers in the juices remaining in the frying pan (skillet).

4 Add the chicken stock, lime juice and rind and cook for a further 5 minutes.

5 Add the chillies, oyster sauce and Worcestershire sauce. Season with salt and pepper to taste.

6 Pour the (bell) peppers and juices over the chicken and onions.

7 Cover the casserole with a lid or cooking foil.

8 Cook in the centre of a preheated oven, 190°C/375°F/Gas Mark 5, for 1½ hours until the chicken is very tender, then serve.

COOK'S TIP

Try this casserole with a cheese scone (biscuit) topping. About 30 minutes before the end of cooking time, simply top with rounds cut from cheese scone (biscuit) pastry.

Bourguignonne of Chicken

A recipe based on a classic French dish. Use a good quality wine when making this casserole.

Serves 4–6

INGREDIENTS

4 tbsp sunflower oil
900 g/1³/₄ lb chicken meat, diced
250 g/9 oz/3 cups button
    mushrooms
125 g/4¹/₂ oz/²/₃ cup rindless,
    smoked bacon, diced
16 shallots

2 garlic cloves, crushed
1 tbsp plain (all-purpose) flour
150 ml/¹/₄ pint/²/₃ cup white
    Burgundy wine
150 ml/¹/₄ pint/²/₃ cup chicken stock

1 bouquet garni (1 bay leaf, sprig
    thyme, stick of celery, parsley and
    sage tied with string)
salt and pepper
deep-fried croûtons and a selection
    of cooked vegetables, to serve

1 Heat the sunflower oil in an ovenproof casserole and brown the chicken all over. Remove from the casserole with a slotted spoon.

2 Add the mushrooms, bacon, shallots and garlic to the casserole and cook for 4 minutes.

3 Return the chicken to the casserole and sprinkle with flour. Cook for a further 2 minutes, stirring.

4 Add the Burgundy wine and chicken stock to the casserole and stir until boiling. Add the bouquet garni and season well with salt and pepper.

5 Cover the casserole and bake in the centre of a preheated oven, 150°C/300°F/Gas Mark 2, for 1¹/₂ hours. Remove the bouquet garni.

6 Deep fry some heart-shaped croûtons (about 8 large ones)

in beef dripping(s) and serve with the bourguignonne.

COOK'S TIP

A good quality red wine can be used instead of the white wine, to produce a rich, glossy red sauce.

Country Chicken Bake

This economical bake is a complete meal – its crusty, herb-flavoured French bread topping mops up the tasty juices, and means there's no need to serve potatoes or rice separately.

Serves 4

INGREDIENTS

2 tbsp sunflower oil
4 chicken quarters
16 small whole onions, peeled
3 sticks (stalks) celery, sliced
400 g/14 oz can red kidney beans
4 medium tomatoes, quartered

200 ml/7 fl oz/ scant 1 cup
    dry cider or stock
4 tbsp chopped fresh parsley
1 tsp paprika
60 g/2 oz/4 tbsp butter
12 slices French bread

salt and pepper

1 Heat the oil in a flameproof casserole and fry the chicken quarters two at a time until golden. Using a slotted spoon, remove the chicken from the pan and set aside until required.

2 Add the onions and fry, turning occasionally, until golden brown. Add the celery and fry for 2–3 minutes. Return the chicken to the pan, then stir in the beans, tomatoes, cider, half the parsley, salt and pepper. Sprinkle with the paprika.

3 Cover and cook in a preheated oven, 200°C/400°F/ Gas Mark 6, for 20–25 minutes, until the chicken juices run clear when pierced with a skewer.

4 Mix the remaining parsley with the butter and spread evenly over the French bread.

5 Uncover the casserole, arrange the bread slices overlapping on top and bake for a further 10–12 minutes, until golden and crisp.

COOK'S TIP

Add a crushed garlic clove to the parsley butter for extra flavour.

VARIATION

For a more Italian-tasting dish, replace the garlic and parsley bread topping with the Pesto Toasts (see page 208).

Hungarian Chicken Goulash

Goulash is traditionally made with beef, but this recipe successfully uses chicken instead. To reduce fat, use a low-fat cream in place of the soured cream.

Serves 6

INGREDIENTS

900 g/1³/₄ lb chicken meat, diced
60 g/2 oz/¹/₂ cup flour, seasoned
   with 1 tsp paprika, salt and pepper
2 tbsp olive oil
25 g/1 oz/2 tbsp butter
1 onion, sliced
24 shallots, peeled

1 each red and green
   (bell) pepper, chopped
1 tbsp paprika
1 tsp rosemary, crushed
4 tbsp tomato purée (paste)
300 ml/¹/₂ pint/1¹/₄ cups
   chicken stock

150 ml/¹/₄ pint/²/₃ cup claret
400 g/14 oz can chopped tomatoes
150 ml/¹/₄ pint/²/₃ cup soured cream
1 tbsp chopped fresh parsley,
   to garnish
chunks of bread and a side salad,
   to serve

1 Toss the chicken in the seasoned flour until it is coated all over.

2 In a flameproof casserole, heat the oil and butter and fry the onion, shallots and (bell) peppers for 3 minutes.

3 Add the chicken and cook for a further 4 minutes.

4 Sprinkle with the paprika and rosemary.

5 Add the tomato purée (paste), chicken stock, claret and chopped tomatoes, cover and cook in the centre of a preheated oven, 160°C/325°F/Gas Mark 3 for 1½ hours.

6 Remove the casserole from the oven, allow it to stand for 4 minutes, then add the soured cream and garnish with parsley.

7 Serve with chunks of bread and a side salad.

VARIATION

Serve the goulash with buttered ribbon noodles instead of bread. For an authentic touch, try a Hungarian red wine instead of the claret.

Country Chicken Braise with Rosemary Dumplings

Root vegetables are always cheap and nutritious, and combined with chicken they make tasty and economical casseroles.

Serves 4

INGREDIENTS

4 chicken quarters
2 tbsp sunflower oil
2 medium leeks
250 g/9 oz/1 cup carrots, chopped
250 g/9 oz/2 cups parsnips, chopped
2 small turnips, chopped

600 ml/1 pint/2$\frac{1}{2}$ cups chicken stock
3 tbsp Worcestershire sauce
2 sprigs fresh rosemary
salt and pepper

DUMPLINGS:
200 g/7 oz/1$\frac{3}{4}$ cups self-raising
  flour
100 g/3$\frac{1}{2}$ oz shredded suet
1 tbsp chopped rosemary leaves
cold water, to mix

1 Remove the skin from the chicken if you prefer. Heat the oil in a large, flameproof casserole or heavy saucepan and fry the chicken until golden. Using a slotted spoon, remove the chicken from the pan. Drain off the excess fat.

2 Trim and slice the leeks. Add the carrots, parsnips and turnips to the casserole and cook for 5 minutes, until lightly coloured. Return the chicken to the pan.

3 Add the chicken stock, Worcestershire sauce, rosemary and seasoning, then bring to the boil.

4 Reduce the heat, cover and simmer gently for about 50 minutes or until the juices run clear when the chicken is pierced with a skewer.

5 To make the dumplings, combine the flour, suet and rosemary leaves with salt and pepper in a bowl. Stir in just enough cold water to bind to a firm dough.

6 Form into 8 small balls and place on top of the chicken and vegetables. Cover and simmer for a further 10–12 minutes, until the dumplings are well risen. Serve with the casserole.

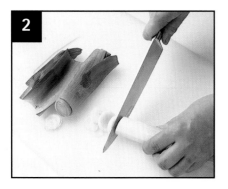

Chicken with Shallots in Wild Mushroom & Ginger Sauce

This recipe has an oriental flavour, which can be further enhanced with chopped spring onions (scallions), cinnamon and lemon grass.

Serves 6-8

INGREDIENTS

6 tbsp sesame oil
900 g/1³/₄ lb chicken meat
60 g/2 oz/¹/₂ cup flour, seasoned
32 shallots, sliced
500 g/1 lb 2 oz/6 cups wild
   mushrooms, roughly chopped

300 ml/¹/₂ pint/1¹/₄ cups chicken
   stock
2 tbsp Worcestershire sauce
1 tbsp honey
2 tbsp grated fresh root ginger
150 ml/¹/₄ pint/²/₃ cup yogurt

salt and pepper
flat leaf parsley, to garnish
wild rice and white rice, to serve

1 Heat the oil in a large frying pan (skillet). Coat the chicken in the seasoned flour and cook for about 4 minutes, until browned all over. Transfer to a large deep casserole and keep warm until required.

2 Slowly fry the shallots and mushrooms in the juices.

3 Add the chicken stock, Worcestershire sauce, honey and fresh ginger, then season to taste with salt and pepper.

4 Pour the mixture over the chicken, and cover the casserole with a lid or cooking foil.

5 Cook in the centre of a preheated oven, 150°C/300°F/ Gas Mark 2, for about 1¹/₂ hours, until the meat is very tender. Add the yogurt and cook for a further 10 minutes. Serve the casserole with a mixture of wild rice and white rice, and garnish with fresh parsley.

COOK'S TIP

Mushrooms can be stored in the refrigerator for 24–36 hours. Keep them in paper bags as they 'sweat' in plastic. You do not need to peel mushrooms but wild mushrooms must be washed thoroughly.

Jamaican Hot Pot

A tasty way to make chicken joints go a long way, this hearty casserole, spiced with the warm, subtle flavour of ginger, is a good choice for a Halloween party.

Serves 4

INGREDIENTS

2 tsp sunflower oil
4 chicken drumsticks
4 chicken thighs
1 medium onion
750 g/1 lb 10 oz piece squash
    or pumpkin, diced
1 green (bell) pepper, sliced

2.5 cm/1 inch fresh ginger root,
    chopped finely
400 g/14 oz can chopped
    tomatoes
300 ml/^{1}/$_2$ pint/1^1/$_4$ cups
    chicken stock

60 g/2 oz/^{1}/$_4$ cup
    split lentils
garlic salt and cayenne pepper
350 g/12 oz can sweetcorn
    (corn-on-the-cob)
crusty bread, to serve

1 Heat the oil in a large flameproof casserole and fry the chicken joints until golden, turning frequently.

2 Using a sharp knife, peel and slice the onion, peel and dice the pumpkin or squash and deseed and slice the (bell) pepper.

3 Drain any excess fat from the pan and add the prepared onion, pumpkin and pepper. Gently fry for a few minutes until lightly browned. Add the chopped ginger, tomatoes, chicken stock and lentils. Season lightly with garlic salt and cayenne pepper.

4 Cover the casserole and place in a preheated oven, 190°C/ 375°F/Gas Mark 5, for about 1 hour, until the vegetables are tender and the chicken juices run clear when pierced with a skewer.

5 Add the drained corn and cook for a further 5 minutes. Season to taste and serve with crusty bread.

VARIATION

If you can't find fresh ginger root, add 1 teaspoon allspice for a warm, fragrant aroma.

VARIATION

If squash or pumpkin is not available, swede (rutabaga) makes a good substitute.

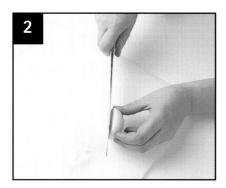

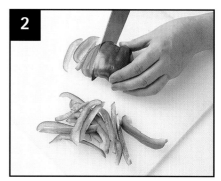

Garlic Chicken Casserole

This is a cassoulet with a twist – it is made with chicken instead of duck and lamb. Save time by using canned beans, such as borlotti or cannellini beans, which are both good in this dish.

Serves 4

INGREDIENTS

4 tbsp sunflower oil
900 g/1³/₄ lb chicken meat, chopped
250 g/9 oz/3 cups mushrooms, sliced
16 shallots
6 garlic cloves, crushed
1 tbsp plain (all-purpose) flour

250 ml/9 fl oz/1 cup white wine
250 ml/9 fl oz/1 cup chicken stock
1 bouquet garni (1 bay leaf, sprig thyme, celery, parsley & sage tied together with string)
400 g/14 oz can borlotti beans

salt and pepper
patty pans, to serve

1 Heat the sunflower oil in an ovenproof casserole and fry the chicken until browned all over. Remove the chicken from the casserole with a slotted spoon and set aside until required.

2 Add the mushrooms, shallots and garlic to the fat in the casserole and cook for 4 minutes.

3 Return the chicken to the casserole and sprinkle with the flour, then cook for a further 2 minutes.

4 Add the white wine and chicken stock, stir until boiling, then add the bouquet garni. Season well with salt and pepper.

5 Drain the borlotti beans and rinse thoroughly, then add to the casserole.

6 Cover and place in the centre of a preheated oven, 150°C/300°F/Gas Mark 2, for 2 hours. Remove the bouquet garni and serve the casserole with patty pans.

COOK'S TIP

Mushrooms are ideal in a low-fat diet because they are high in flavour and contain no fat. Experiment with the wealth of varieties that are now available from supermarkets.

COOK'S TIP

Serve the casserole with wholemeal (whole wheat) rice to make this filling dish go even further.

Old English Chicken Stewed in Ale

This is a slow-cooked, old-fashioned stew to warm up a wintery day. The rarebit toasts are a perfect accompaniment to soak up the rich juices, but if you prefer, serve the stew with jacket potatoes.

Serves 4-6

INGREDIENTS

4 large, skinless chicken thighs
2 tbsp plain (all-purpose) flour
2 tbsp English mustard powder
2 tbsp sunflower oil
15 g/$^1/_2$ oz/1 tbsp butter
4 small onions
600 ml/1 pint/2$^1/_2$ cups beer

2 tbsp Worcestershire sauce
3 tbsp chopped fresh sage leaves
salt and pepper

RAREBIT TOASTS:
60 g/2 oz/$^1/_2$ cup grated mature
  English Cheddar

1 tsp English mustard powder
1 tsp plain (all-purpose) flour
1 tsp Worcestershire sauce
1 tbsp beer
2 slices wholemeal (whole wheat)
  toast

1 Trim any excess fat from the chicken and toss in the flour and mustard powder to coat evenly. Heat the sunflower oil and butter in a large flameproof casserole and fry the chicken over a fairly high heat, turning occasionally, until golden. Remove the chicken from the casserole with a slotted spoon and keep hot.

2 Peel the onions and slice into wedges, then fry quickly until golden. Add the chicken, beer, Worcestershire sauce, fresh sage, and salt and pepper to taste. Bring to the boil, cover and simmer very gently for about 1½ hours, until the chicken is very tender.

3 Meanwhile, make the rarebit toasts: mix the cheese with the mustard powder, flour, Worcestershire sauce and beer. Spread the mixture over the toasts and cook under a hot grill (broiler) for about 1 minute, until melted and golden. Cut into triangles.

4 Stir the sage leaves into the chicken stew, bring to the boil and serve with the rarebit toasts, a green vegetable and new potatoes.

COOK'S TIP

If you do not have fresh sage, use 2 tsp of dried sage in step 2.

Brittany Chicken Casserole

A hearty, one-dish meal that would make a substantial lunch or supper. As it requires a long cooking time, make double quantities and freeze half to eat later.

Serves 6

INGREDIENTS

500 g/1 lb 2 oz/2^1/$_2$ cups beans, such as flageolets, soaked overnight and drained
25 g/1 oz/2 tbsp butter
2 tbsp olive oil
3 rindless bacon slices, chopped

900 g/1^3/$_4$ lb chicken pieces
1 tbsp plain (all-purpose) flour
300 ml/^{1}/$_2$ pint/1^1/$_4$ cups cider
150 ml/^{1}/$_4$ pint/^{2}/$_3$ cup chicken stock
14 shallots
2 tbsp honey, warmed

250 g/8 oz ready-cooked beetroot
salt and pepper

1 Cook the beans in salted boiling water for about 25 minutes.

2 Heat the butter and olive oil in a flameproof casserole, add the bacon and chicken and cook for 5 minutes.

3 Sprinkle with the flour then add the cider and chicken stock, stirring constantly to avoid lumps forming. Season with salt and pepper to taste and bring to the boil.

4 Add the beans then cover the casserole tightly with a lid or cooking foil and bake in the centre of a preheated oven, 160°C/325°F/ Gas Mark 3, for 2 hours.

5 About 15 minutes before the end of cooking time, remove the lid or cooking foil from the casserole.

6 In a frying pan (skillet), gently cook the shallots and honey together for 5 minutes, turning the shallots frequently.

7 Add the shallots and cooked beetroot to the casserole and leave to finish cooking in the oven for the last 15 minutes.

COOK'S TIP

To save time, use canned flageolet beans instead of dried. Drain and rinse before adding to the chicken.

Rich Mediterranean Chicken Casserole

A colourful casserole packed with sunshine flavours from the Mediterranean.
Sun-dried tomatoes add a wonderful richness and you need very few to make this dish really special.

Serves 4

INGREDIENTS

8 chicken thighs
2 tbsp olive oil
1 medium red onion, sliced
2 garlic cloves, crushed
1 large red (bell) pepper, sliced thickly
thinly pared rind and juice
    of 1 small orange
125 ml/4 floz/^{1}/$_{2}$ cup chicken stock

400 g/14 oz can chopped tomatoes
25 g/1 oz/^{1}/$_{2}$ cup sun-dried
    tomatoes, thinly sliced
1 tbsp chopped fresh thyme
50 g/1^{3}/$_{4}$ oz/^{1}/$_{2}$ cup pitted black
    olives

salt and pepper
thyme sprigs and orange
    rind, to garnish
crusty fresh bread, to serve

1 In a heavy or non-stick large frying pan (skillet), fry the chicken without fat over a fairly high heat, turning occasionally until golden brown. Using a slotted spoon, drain off any excess fat from the chicken and transfer to a flameproof casserole.

2 Fry the onion, garlic and (bell) pepper in the pan over a moderate heat for 3–4 minutes. Transfer to the casserole.

3 Add the orange rind and juice, chicken stock, canned tomatoes and sun-dried tomatoes and stir to combine.

4 Bring to the boil then cover the casserole with a lid and simmer very gently over a low heat for about 1 hour, stirring occasionally. Add the chopped fresh thyme and pitted black olives, then adjust the seasoning with salt and pepper.

5 Scatter orange rind and thyme over the casserole to garnish, and serve with crusty bread.

COOK'S TIP

Sun-dried tomatoes have a dense texture and concentrated taste, and add intense flavour to slow-cooking casseroles.

Chicken Madeira "French-style"

Madeira is a fortified wine which can be used in both sweet and savoury dishes. Here it adds a rich, full flavour to the casserole.

Serves 8

INGREDIENTS

25 g/1 oz/2 tbsp butter
20 baby onions
250 g/9 oz/1¹/₂ cups carrots, sliced
250 g/9 oz/1¹/₂ cups bacon, chopped
250 g/9 oz/3 cups button
   mushrooms

1 chicken, weighing about 1.5 kg/
   3 lb 5 oz
425 ml/15 fl oz/1⁷/₈ cups white wine
25 g/1 oz/¹/₄ cup seasoned flour
425ml/15 fl oz/1⁷/₈ cups chicken
   stock

bouquet garni
150 ml/¹/₄ pint/²/₃ cup Madeira wine
salt and pepper
mashed potato or pasta, to serve

1 Heat the butter in a large frying pan (skillet) and fry the onions, carrots, bacon and button mushrooms for 3 minutes, stirring frequently. Transfer to a large casserole dish.

2 Add the chicken to the frying pan (skillet) and brown all over. Transfer to the casserole dish with the vegetables and bacon.

3 Add the white wine and cook until the wine is nearly completely reduced.

4 Sprinkle with the seasoned flour, stirring to avoid lumps from forming.

5 Add the chicken stock, salt and pepper to taste and the bouquet garni. Cover and cook the casserole for 2 hours. About 30 minutes before the end of cooking time, add the Madeira wine and continue cooking uncovered.

6 Carve the chicken and serve with mashed potato or pasta.

COOK'S TIP

You can add any combination of herbs to this recipe – chervil is a popular herb in French cuisine, but add it at the end of cooking so that its delicate flavour is not lost. Other herbs which work well with chicken are parsley and tarragon.

Springtime Chicken Cobbler

Fresh spring vegetables are the basis of this colourful casserole, which is topped with hearty wholemeal (whole wheat) dumplings for a complete, healthy family meal.

Serves 4

INGREDIENTS

8 skinless chicken drumsticks
1 tbsp oil
1 small onion, sliced
350 g/12 oz/1$^{1}/_{2}$ cups baby carrots
2 baby turnips
125 g/4$^{1}/_{2}$ oz/1 cup broad beans or peas
1 tsp cornflour (cornstarch)

300 ml/$^{1}/_{2}$ pint/1$^{1}/_{4}$ cups chicken stock
2 bay leaves
salt and pepper

COBBLER TOPPING:
250 g/9 oz/2 cups wholemeal (whole wheat) plain flour

2 tsp baking powder
25 g/1 oz/2 tbsp sunflower soft margarine
2 tsp dry wholegrain mustard
60 g/2 oz/$^{1}/_{2}$ cup Cheddar cheese, grated
skimmed milk, to mix
sesame seeds, to sprinkle

1 Fry the chicken in the oil, turning, until golden brown. Drain well and place in an ovenproof casserole. Sauté the onion for 2–3 minutes to soften.

2 Wash and trim the carrots and turnips and cut into equal-sized pieces. Add to the casserole with the onions and beans or peas.

3 Blend the cornflour (cornstarch) with a little of the stock, then stir in the rest and heat gently, stirring until boiling. Pour into the casserole and add the bay leaves, salt and pepper.

4 Cover tightly and bake in a preheated oven, 200°C/400°F/ Gas Mark 6, for 50–60 minutes, or until the chicken juices run clear when pierced with a skewer.

5 For the topping, sift the flour and baking powder. Mix in the margarine with a fork. Stir in the mustard, the cheese and enough milk to form a fairly soft dough.

6 Roll out and cut 16 rounds with a 4 cm/1½ inch cutter. Uncover the casserole, arrange the scone (biscuit) rounds on top, then brush with milk and sprinkle with sesame seeds. Bake in the oven for 20 minutes or until the topping is golden and firm.

Californian Chicken

*It is better if you have time to bone the chicken completely,
or use chicken breast after removing all the fat and skin.*

Serves 4–6

INGREDIENTS

175 g/6 oz/1^1/$_2$ cups plain
  (all-purpose) flour
1 tsp paprika
1 tsp freeze-dried Italian seasoning
1 tsp freeze-dried tarragon
1 tsp rosemary, finely crushed
2 eggs, beaten

120 ml/4 fl oz/^{1}/$_2$ cup milk
1 chicken, weighing about
  2 kg/4 lb, jointed
seasoned flour
150 ml/^{1}/$_4$ pint/^{2}/$_3$ cup rapeseed oil
2 bananas, quartered
1 apple, cut into rings,

350 g/12 oz can sweetcorn (corn-on-
  the-cob) & peppers, drained
oil for frying
salt and pepper
peppercorn or horseradish sauce,
  to serve

1 Mix together the flour, spices, herbs and a pinch of salt in a large bowl. Make a well in the centre and add the eggs.

2 Blend and slowly add the milk, whisking until very smooth.

3 Coat the chicken pieces with seasoned flour and dip the chicken pieces into the batter mix.

4 Heat the oil in a large frying pan (skillet). Add the chicken and fry for about 3 minutes or until lightly browned all over. Place the chicken pieces on a non-stick baking tray (cookie sheet).

5 Batter the bananas and apple rings and fry for 2 minutes.

6 Finally toss the sweetcorn (corn-on-the-cob) into the leftover batter.

7 Heat a little oil in a frying pan (skillet). Drop in spoonfuls of the sweetcorn mixture to make flat patty cakes. Cook for 4 minutes on each side. Keep warm with the apple and banana fritters.

8 Bake the chicken in a preheated oven, 200°C/400°F/Gas Mark 6, for about 25 minutes until the chicken is tender and golden brown.

9 Arrange the chicken, sweetcorn fritters, and the apple and banana fritters on a bed of fresh watercress. Serve with a peppercorn or horseradish sauce.

Chicken with Baby Onions & Green Peas

Pork fat adds a tasty flavour to this dish. If you can't find fresh garden peas, frozen peas are a good substitute.

Serves 4

INGREDIENTS

250 g/9 oz/1 cup pork fat, cut into small cubes
60 g/2 oz/4 tbsp butter
16 small onions or shallots

1 kg/2 lb 4 oz boneless chicken pieces
25 g/1 oz/¼ cup plain (all-purpose) flour
600 ml/1 pint/2½ cups chicken stock

bouquet garni
500 g/1 lb 2 oz/4 cups fresh peas
salt and pepper

1 Bring a saucepan of salted water to the boil and simmer the pork fat cubes for three minutes. Drain and dry the pork on absorbent paper towels.

2 Melt the butter in a large frying pan (skillet), add the pork and onions, fry gently for 3 minutes until lightly browned.

3 Remove the pork and onions from the pan and set aside until required. Add the chicken pieces to the pan and cook until browned all over. Transfer the chicken to an ovenproof casserole.

4 Add the flour to the pan and cook, stirring until it begins to brown, then slowly blend in the chicken stock.

5 Cook the chicken, with the sauce and bouquet garni, in a preheated oven, 200°C/400°F/Gas Mark 6, for 35 minutes.

6 Remove the bouquet garni about 10 minutes before the end of cooking time and add the peas and the reserved pork and onions. Stir to mix.

7 When cooked, place the chicken pieces on to a large platter, surrounded with the pork, peas and onions.

COOK'S TIP

If you want to cut down on fat, use lean bacon, cut into small cubes, rather than pork fat.

Festive Apple Chicken

*The richly flavoured stuffing in this recipe is cooked under the breast skin of the chicken,
so not only is all the flavour sealed in, but the chicken stays really moist and succulent during cooking.*

Serves 6

INGREDIENTS

1 chicken, weighing 2 kg/ 4 lb
2 dessert apples
15 g/$^1/_2$ oz/1 tbsp butter
1 tbsp redcurrant jelly
mixed vegetables, to serve

STUFFING:
15 g/$^1/_2$ oz/1 tbsp butter
1 small onion, chopped finely
60 g/2 oz mushrooms, chopped finely
60 g/2 oz smoked ham,
  chopped finely
25 g/1 oz/$^1/_2$ cup fresh breadcrumbs

1 tbsp chopped fresh parsley
1 crisp eating apple
1 tbsp lemon juice
oil, for brushing
salt and pepper

1 To make the stuffing, melt the butter and fry the onion gently, stirring until softened but not browned. Stir in the mushrooms and cook for 2–3 minutes. Remove from the heat and stir in the ham, breadcrumbs and the chopped parsley.

2 Core the apple, leaving the skin on, and grate coarsely. Add the stuffing mixture to the apple with the lemon juice. Season to taste.

3 Loosen the breast skin of the chicken and carefully spoon the stuffing mixture under it, smoothing the skin over evenly with your hands.

4 Place the chicken in a roasting tin (pan) and brush lightly with oil.

5 Roast the chicken in a preheated oven, 190°C/375°F/ Gas Mark 5, for 25 minutes per 500 g/1 lb plus 25 minutes, or until

there is no trace of pink in the juices when the chicken is pierced through the thickest part with a skewer. If the breast starts to brown too much, cover the chicken with foil.

6 Core and slice the remaining apples and sauté in the butter until golden. Stir in the redcurrant jelly and warm through until melted. Garnish the chicken with the apple slices and serve with mixed vegetables.

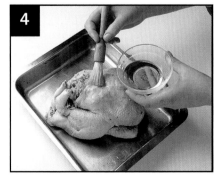

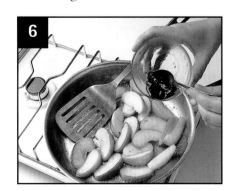

Roast Chicken with Coriander (Cilantro) & Garlic

This recipe for chicken is coated with a fresh-flavoured marinade then roasted. Try serving it with rice, yogurt and salad.

Serves 4–6

INGREDIENTS

3 sprigs fresh coriander (cilantro), chopped
4 garlic cloves
1/2 tsp salt

1 tsp pepper
4 tbsp lemon juice
4 tbsp olive oil
1 large chicken

pepper
sprig of fresh parsley, to garnish
boiled potatoes and carrots, to serve

1 Place the chopped coriander (cilantro), garlic, salt, pepper, lemon juice and olive oil in a pestle and mortar and pound together or blend in a food processor. Chill for 4 hours to allow the flavours to develop.

2 Place the chicken in a roasting tin (pan). Coat generously with the coriander and garlic mixture.

3 Sprinkle with pepper and roast in a preheated oven, 190°C/375°F/Gas Mark 5, on a low shelf for 1½ hours, basting every 20 minutes with the coriander mixture. If the chicken starts to turn brown, cover with foil. Garnish with fresh parsley and serve with the potatoes and carrots.

COOK'S TIP

For pounding small quantities it is best to use a pestle and mortar so as little as possible of the mixture is left in the container.

VARIATION

Any fresh herb can be used in this recipe instead of the coriander (cilantro). Tarragon or thyme are a good combination with chicken.

Feta Chicken with Mountain Herbs

Chicken goes well with most savoury herbs, especially during the summer, when fresh herbs are at their best. This combination makes a good partner for tangy feta cheese and sun-ripened tomatoes.

Serves 4

INGREDIENTS

8 skinless, boneless chicken thighs
2 tbsp each chopped fresh thyme, rosemary and oregano
125 g/4^1/$_2$ oz feta cheese
1 tbsp milk
2 tbsp plain (all-purpose) flour
salt and pepper

thyme, rosemary and oregano, to garnish

TOMATO SAUCE:
1 medium onion, roughly chopped
1 garlic clove, crushed
1 tbsp olive oil
4 medium plum tomatoes, quartered

sprig each of thyme, rosemary and oregano

1 Spread out the chicken thighs on a board, smooth side downwards.

2 Divide the herbs among the chicken thighs, then cut the cheese into eight sticks. Place one stick of cheese in the centre of each chicken thigh. Season well, then roll up to enclose the cheese.

3 Place the rolls in an ovenproof dish, brush with milk and dust with flour to coat evenly.

4 Bake in a preheated oven, 190°C/375°F/Gas Mark 5, for 25–30 minutes, or until golden brown. The juices should run clear and not pink when the chicken is pierced with a skewer in the thickest part.

5 To make the sauce, cook the onion and garlic in the olive oil, stirring, until softened and beginning to brown.

6 Add the tomatoes, reduce the heat, cover and simmer gently for 15–20 minutes or until soft.

7 Add the herbs, then transfer to a food processor and blend to a purée. Press through a sieve to make a smooth, rich sauce. Season to taste and serve the sauce with the chicken, garnished with herbs.

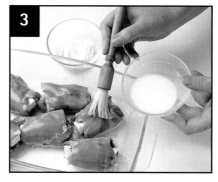

Poussin with Dried Fruits

Baby chickens are ideal for a one or two portion meal, and cook very easily and quickly for a special dinner. If you're cooking for one, a microwave makes cooking even quicker and more convenient.

Serves 2

INGREDIENTS

125 g/4^1/2 oz/^{3}/4 cup dried apples,
   peaches and prunes
120 ml/4 fl oz/^{1}/2 cup
   boiling water
2 baby chickens

25 g/1 oz/^{1}/3 cup walnut halves
1 tbsp honey
1 tsp ground allspice
1 tbsp walnut oil

salt and pepper
fresh vegetables and new potatoes,
   to serve

1 Place the dried fruits in a bowl, cover with the boiling water and leave to stand for about 30 minutes.

2 Cut the chickens in half down the breastbone using a sharp knife, or leave them whole, if you prefer.

3 Mix the fruit and any juices remaining in the bowl with the walnut halves, honey and ground allspice and divide the mixture between two small roasting bags or squares of foil.

4 Brush the chickens with walnut oil and sprinkle with salt and pepper then place on top of the fruits.

5 Close the roasting bags or fold the foil over to enclose the chickens and bake on a baking tray (cookie sheet) in a preheated oven, 190°C/375°F/Gas Mark 5, for 25–30 minutes or until the juices run clear and not pink when the chicken is pierced in the thickest part with a skewer. To cook in a microwave, use microwave roasting bags and cook on high/100% power for 6–7 minutes each, depending on size.

6 Serve hot with fresh vegetables and new potatoes.

COOK'S TIP

Alternative dried fruits that can be used in this recipe are cherries, mangoes or pawpaws.

Chicken with Marmalade Stuffing

Marmalade lovers will enjoy this festive recipe. You can use any favourite marmalade, such as lemon or grapefruit.

Serves 6

INGREDIENTS

1 chicken, weighing about 2.25 kg/5 lb
bay leaves

STUFFING:
1 stick (stalk) celery, chopped finely
1 small onion, chopped finely
1 tbsp sunflower oil

125 g/4^1/$_2$ oz/2 cups fresh
 wholemeal (whole wheat)
 breadcrumbs
4 tbsp marmalade
2 tbsp chopped fresh parsley
1 egg, beaten
salt and pepper

SAUCE:
2 tsp cornflour (cornstarch)
2 tbsp orange juice
3 tbsp marmalade
150 ml/^{1}/$_4$ pint/^{2}/$_3$ cup chicken stock
1 medium orange
2 tbsp brandy

1 Lift the neck flap of the chicken and remove the wishbone using a small, sharp knife. Place a sprig of bay leaves inside the body cavity.

2 For the stuffing, sauté the celery and onion in the oil to soften. Add the breadcrumbs, 3 tablespoons of marmalade, parsley and egg. Season and use to stuff the neck cavity of the chicken. Any extra stuffing may be cooked separately.

3 Place the chicken in a roasting tin (pan) and brush lightly with oil. Roast in a preheated oven, 190°C/375°F/Gas Mark 5 for 20 minutes per 500 g/1 lb 2 oz plus 20 minutes or until the juices run clear when the chicken is pierced in the thickest part with a skewer. Remove from the oven and glaze with the remaining marmalade.

4 Meanwhile, to make the sauce, blend the cornflour (cornstarch) in a pan with the orange juice, then add the marmalade and chicken stock. Heat gently, stirring, until thickened and smooth. Remove from the heat. Cut the segments from the orange, discarding all white pith and membrane. Just before serving, add the orange segments and brandy to the sauce and bring to the boil.

5 Serve the chicken with the orange sauce, any extra stuffing and new potatoes.

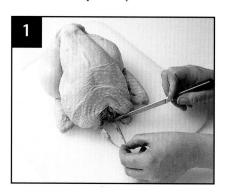

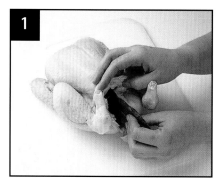

Golden Chicken with Mango & Cranberries

This recipe, which uses a partly-boned chicken is easy to slice and serve. If you prefer, stuff in the traditional way at the neck end, and cook any remaining stuffing separately.

Serves 6

INGREDIENTS

1 chicken, weighing about 2.25 kg/5 lb
6 slices smoked bacon

STUFFING:
1 ripe mango, diced
60g/2 oz/$^1/_4$ cup fresh or frozen
    cranberries

125 g/4$^1/_2$ oz/2 cups breadcrumbs
$^1/_2$ tsp ground mace
1 egg, beaten
salt and pepper

GLAZE:
$^1/_2$ tsp ground turmeric
2 tsp honey
2 tsp sunflower oil

1 To part-bone the chicken, dislocate the legs and place the chicken breast-side downwards. Cut a straight line through the skin along the ridge of the back. Scrape the meat down from the bone on both sides.

2 When you reach the point where the legs and wings join the body, cut through the joints. Work around the ribcage until the carcass can be lifted away.

3 Make six bacon rolls. For the stuffing, mix the mango with the cranberries, breadcrumbs and mace, then bind with egg. Season.

4 Place the chicken, skin-side down, and spoon over half the stuffing. Arrange the bacon rolls down the centre then top with the remaining stuffing. Fold the skin over and tie with string. Turn the chicken over, truss the legs and tuck the wings underneath. Place

in a roasting tin (pan). To make the glaze, mix the turmeric, honey and oil and brush over the skin.

5 Roast in a preheated oven, 190°C/375°F/Gas Mark 5, for 1$^1/_2$–2 hours or until the juices run clear, not pink, when the chicken is pierced with a skewer. When the chicken starts to brown, cover loosely with foil to prevent overbrowning. Serve the chicken hot with seasonal vegetables.

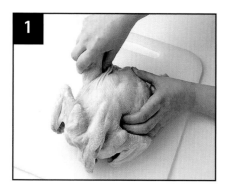

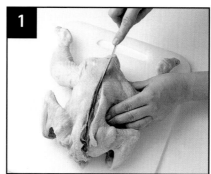

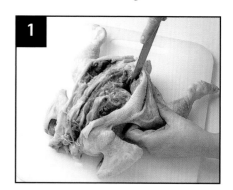

Roast Chicken Breasts with Bacon & Dripping(s) Triangles

Chicken suprêmes have a little bit of the wing bone remaining which makes them easy to pick up and eat. In this recipe, a tart, fruity sauce perfectly complements the chicken and dripping(s) triangles.

Serves 8

INGREDIENTS

60 g/2 oz/4 tbsp butter
juice of 1 lemon
250 g/9 oz/1 cup redcurrants or
  cranberries

1–2 tbsp muscovado sugar
8 chicken suprêmes or breasts
16 slices of streaky bacon
thyme

60 g/2 oz/4 tbsp beef dripping(s)
4 slices of bread, cut into triangles
salt and pepper

1 Heat the butter in a saucepan, add the lemon juice, redcurrants or cranberries, muscovado sugar and salt and pepper to taste. Cook for 1 minute and allow to cool until required.

2 Meanwhile, season the chicken with salt and pepper. Wrap 2 slices of streaky bacon around each breast and sprinkle with thyme.

3 Wrap each breast in a piece of lightly greased foil and place in a roasting tin (pan). Roast in a preheated oven, 200°C/400°F/Gas Mark 6, for 15 minutes. Remove the foil and roast for another 10 minutes.

4 Heat the dripping(s) in a frying pan (skillet), add the bread triangles and fry on both sides until golden brown.

5 Arrange the triangles on a large serving plate and top each with a chicken breast. Serve with a spoonful of the fruit sauce.

COOK'S TIP

You can use either chopped fresh thyme or dried thyme in this recipe, but remember that dried herbs have a stronger flavour so you only need half the quantity compared to fresh herbs.

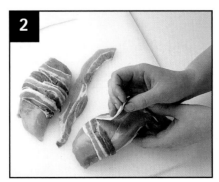

Pollo Catalan

The Catalan region of Spain is famous for its wonderful combinations of meat with fruit. In this recipe, peaches lend a touch of sweetness and pine nuts, cinnamon and sherry add an unusual twist.

Serves 6

INGREDIENTS

60 g/2 oz/1 cup fresh
   brown breadcrumbs
60 g/2 oz/$^1/_2$ cup pine nuts
1 small egg, beaten
4 tbsp chopped fresh thyme
   or 1 tbsp dried thyme

4 fresh peaches or
   8 canned peach halves
1 chicken, weighing about
   2.5 kg/5$^1/_2$ lb
1 tsp ground cinnamon

200 ml/7 fl oz/$^3/_4$ cup
   Amontillado sherry
4 tbsp double (heavy) cream
salt and pepper

1 Combine the breadcrumbs with 25 g/1 oz/$^1/_4$ cup pine nuts, the egg and the thyme.

2 Halve and stone the peaches, removing the skin if necessary. Dice one peach into small pieces and stir into the breadcrumb mixture. Season well. Spoon the stuffing into the neck cavity of the chicken, securing the skin firmly over it.

3 Place the chicken in a roasting tin (pan). Sprinkle the cinnamon over the skin.

4 Cover loosely with foil and roast in a preheated oven, 190°C/375°F/Gas Mark 5, for 1 hour, basting occasionally.

5 Remove the foil and spoon the sherry over the chicken. Cook for a further 30 minutes, basting with the sherry, until the juices run clear when the chicken is pierced in the thickest part with a skewer.

6 Sprinkle the remaining pine nuts over the remaining peach halves and place in an ovenproof dish in the oven for the final 10 minutes of cooking time.

7 Lift the chicken on to a serving plate and arrange the peach halves around it. Skim any fat from the juices, stir in the cream and heat gently. Serve with the chicken.

COOK'S TIP

Canned apricot halves in natural juice make an easy store-cupboard alternative.

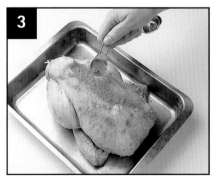

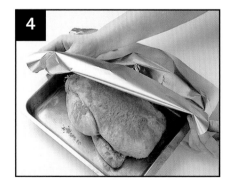

Suprême of Chicken with Black Cherries

This recipe is rather time-consuming but it is well worth the effort.
Cherries and chicken make a good flavour combination.

Serves 6

INGREDIENTS

6 large chicken suprêmes
6 black peppercorns, crushed
300 g/10^1/$_2$ oz/2 cups pitted black
   cherries, or canned pitted cherries
12 shallots, sliced

4 slices rindless, streaky bacon,
   chopped
8 juniper berries
4 tbsp port
150 ml/^{1}/$_4$ pint/^{2}/$_3$ cup red wine
25 g/1 oz/2 tbsp butter

2 tbsp walnut oil
25 g/1 oz/^{1}/$_4$ cup flour
salt and pepper
new potatoes and green beans,
   to serve

1 Place the chicken in an ovenproof dish. Add the peppercorns, cherries or canned cherries, and their juice, if using, and the shallots.

2 Add the bacon, juniper berries, port and red wine. Season well.

3 Place the chicken in the refrigerator and leave to marinate for 48 hours.

4 Heat the butter and walnut oil in a large frying pan (skillet). Remove the chicken from the marinade and fry quickly in the pan for 4 minutes on each side.

5 Return the chicken to the marinade, reserving the butter, oil and juices in the pan.

6 Cover with foil and bake in a preheated oven, 180°C/350°F/ Gas Mark 4, for 20 minutes.

Transfer the chicken from the baking tin (pan) to a warm serving dish. Add the flour to the juices in the frying pan (skillet) and cook for 4 minutes, add the marinade and bring to the boil then simmer for 10 minutes until the sauce reaches a smooth consistency.

7 Pour the cherry sauce over the chicken suprêmes and serve with new potatoes and green beans.

Whisky Roast Chicken

An unusual change from a plain roast, with a distinctly warming Scottish flavour and a delicious oatmeal stuffing.

Serves 6

INGREDIENTS

1 chicken, weighing 2 kg/4 lb 8 oz
oil, for brushing
1 tbsp heather honey
2 tbsp Scotch whisky
2 tbsp plain (all-purpose) flour
300 ml/^{1}/$_2$ pint/1^1/$_4$ cups
  chicken stock

STUFFING:
1 medium onion, finely chopped
1 stick (stalk) celery, sliced thinly
1 tbsp butter or sunflower oil
1 tsp dried thyme
4 tbsp porridge oats
4 tbsp chicken stock

salt and pepper
a green vegetable and sautéed
  potatoes, to serve

1 To make the stuffing, fry the onion and celery in the butter or oil, stirring over a moderate heat until softened and lightly browned.

2 Remove from the heat and stir in the thyme, oats, stock, salt and pepper.

3 Stuff the neck end of the chicken with the mixture and tuck the neck flap under. Place in a roasting tin (pan), brush lightly with oil, and roast in a preheated oven, 190°C/375°F/Gas Mark 5, for about 1 hour.

4 Mix the heather honey with 1 tablespoon whisky and brush the mixture over the chicken. Return to the oven for a further 20 minutes, or until the chicken is golden brown and the juices run clear when the chicken is pierced through the thickest part with a skewer.

5 Lift the chicken on to a serving plate. Skim the fat from the juices then stir in the flour. Stir over a moderate heat until the mixture starts to bubble, then gradually add the stock and remaining whisky.

6 Bring to the boil, stirring, then simmer for 1 minute and serve the chicken with the sauce, a green vegetable and sautéed potatoes.

Roast Chicken in Wild Mushroom Sauce

This unusual chicken dish has the flavour of roast chicken but is finished off in a casserole with a wild mushroom sauce.

Serves 4

INGREDIENTS

90 g/3 oz/^{1}/$_3$ cup butter, softened
1 garlic clove, crushed
1 large chicken
175 g/6 oz/2^1/$_4$ cups wild
   mushrooms
12 shallots

25 g/1 oz/2 tbsp plain (all-purpose)
   flour
150 ml/^{1}/$_4$ pint/^{2}/$_3$ cup brandy
300 ml/^{1}/$_2$ pint/1^1/$_4$ cups double
   (heavy) cream
salt and pepper

1 tbsp chopped fresh parsley,
   to garnish
wild rice or roast potatoes, and green
   beans, to serve

1 Place the butter, garlic, and salt and pepper in a bowl and combine well.

2 Rub the mixture inside and outside of the chicken and leave for 2 hours.

3 Place the chicken in a large roasting tin (pan) and roast in the centre of a preheated oven, 230°C/450°F/Gas Mark 8, for 1½ hours, basting with the garlic butter every ten minutes.

4 Remove the chicken from the roasting tin (pan) and set aside to cool slightly.

5 Transfer the chicken juices to a saucepan and cook the mushrooms and shallots for 5 minutes. Sprinkle with the flour. Add the warm brandy and ignite using a taper or long match.

6 Add the double (heavy) cream and cook for 3 minutes on a very low heat, stirring all the time.

7 Remove the bones and cut the chicken into small bite-sized pieces, then place the meat in a casserole dish. Cover with the mushroom sauce and bake in the oven, with the heat reduced to 160°C/325°F/Gas Mark 3, for a further 12 minutes. Garnish with the parsley and serve with wild rice or roast potatoes, and green beans.

Honeyed Citrus Chicken

This fat-free recipe is great for summer entertaining served simply with a green salad and new potatoes. If you cut the chicken in half and press it flat, you can roast it in under an hour.

Serves 4

INGREDIENTS

2 kg/4 lb 8 oz chicken
salt and pepper
tarragon sprigs, to garnish

MARINADE:
300 ml/^{1}/$_2$ pint/1^1/$_4$ cups orange
   juice
3 tbsp cider vinegar

3 tbsp clear honey
2 tbsp chopped fresh tarragon
2 oranges, cut into wedges

SAUCE:
handful of tarragon sprigs, chopped
200 g/7 oz/1 cup fat-free fromage
   frais

2 tbsp orange juice
1 tsp clear honey
60 g/2 oz/^{1}/$_2$ cup stuffed olives,
   chopped

1 Put the chicken on a chopping board with the breast downwards. Cut through the bottom part of the carcass using poultry shears or heavy kitchen scissors, making sure not to cut right through to the breast bone below.

2 Rinse the chicken with cold water, drain and place on a board with the skin side uppermost. Press the chicken flat, then cut off the leg ends.

3 Thread two long wooden skewers through the bird to keep it flat. Season the skin.

4 Put all the marinade ingredients, except the orange wedges, in a shallow, non-metallic dish. Mix, then add the chicken. Cover and chill for 4 hours, turning the chicken several times.

5 To make the sauce, mix all the ingredients and season. Spoon into a serving dish, cover and chill.

6 Transfer the chicken and marinade to a roasting tin (pan), open out the chicken and place skin-side downwards. Tuck the orange wedges around the chicken and roast in a preheated oven, 200°C/400°F/Gas Mark 6, for 25 minutes. Turn the chicken over and roast for another 20–30 minutes. Baste until the chicken is browned and the juices run clear when pierced with a skewer. Garnish with tarragon and serve with the sauce.

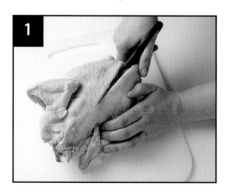

Breast of Chicken with York Ham & Stilton Cheese

Beetroot is one of the most underrated vegetables, adding flavour and colour to numerous dishes. Tender young beetroot are used in this recipe.

Serves 4

INGREDIENTS

4 chicken suprêmes
8 fresh sage leaves
8 thin slices of York ham
250 g/9 oz/2 cups Stilton cheese,
    cut into 8 slices

8 slices rindless streaky bacon
150 ml/1¼ pint/⅔ cup chicken
    stock
2 tbsp port
24 shallots

500 g/1 lb 2 oz baby beetroot, cooked
1 tbsp cornflour (cornstarch),
    blended with a little port
salt and pepper

1 Cut a long slit horizontally along each chicken breast to make a pocket.

2 Insert 2 sage leaves into each pocket and season lightly.

3 Wrap each slice of ham around a slice of cheese and place 2 into each chicken pocket. Carefully wrap enough bacon around each breast to completely cover the pockets containing the ham and the cheese.

4 Place the breasts in an ovenproof casserole dish and pour over the stock and port.

5 Add the shallots, cover with a lid or cooking foil and braise in a preheated oven, 190°C/375°F/Gas Mark 5, for about 40 minutes.

6 Carefully place each breast on to a cutting board and slice through them to create a fan effect. Serve them on a warm serving dish with the shallots and beetroot.

7 Put the juices from the casserole into a saucepan and bring to the boil, remove from the heat and add the cornflour paste. Gently simmer and cook the sauce for 2 minutes, then pour over the shallots and beetroot.

VARIATION

Use any blue-veined cheese instead of the Stilton, if you prefer. Try Gorgonzola or Roquefort.

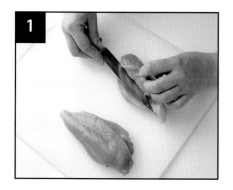

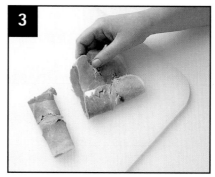

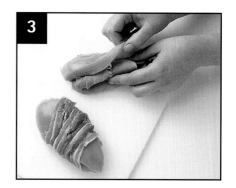

Springtime Roast Chicken

Baby chickens are simple to prepare, take about 30 minutes to roast and can be easily cut in half lengthways with a sharp knife. One baby chicken makes a substantial serving for each person.

Serves 4

INGREDIENTS

5 tbsp fresh brown breadcrumbs
200 g/7 oz/^{1}/$_2$ cup fromage frais
  or low-fat crème fraîche
5 tbsp chopped fresh parsley
5 tbsp chopped fresh chives
4 baby chickens
1 tbsp sunflower oil

675 g/1^1/$_2$ lb young spring
  vegetables such as carrots,
  courgettes (zucchini), sugar snap
  peas, corn (corn-on-the-cob)
  and turnips, cut into small chunks
120 ml/4 fl oz/^{1}/$_2$ cup boiling
  chicken stock

2 tsp cornflour (cornstarch)
150 ml/^{1}/$_4$ pint/^{2}/$_3$ cup
  dry white wine
salt and pepper

1 In a bowl, mix together the breadcrumbs, one-third of the fromage frais or low-fat crème fraîche and 2 tablespoons each of parsley and chives. Season well with salt and pepper then spoon into the neck ends of the baby chickens. Place the chickens on a rack in a roasting tin (pan), brush with oil and season well.

2 Roast in a preheated oven, 220°C/425°F/Gas Mark 7, for 30–35 minutes or until the juices

run clear, not pink, when the chickens are pierced with a skewer.

3 Place the vegetables in a shallow ovenproof dish in one layer and add half the remaining herbs with the chicken stock. Cover and bake for 25–30 minutes until tender. Strain the vegetables, reserving the cooking juices, and keep warm.

4 Lift the chickens on to a serving plate and skim any fat

from the juices in the tin (pan). Add the reserved vegetable juices.

5 Blend the cornflour (cornstarch) with the wine and whisk into the sauce with the remaining fromage frais or low-fat crème fraîche. Whisk until boiling, then add the remaining herbs. Season to taste. Spoon the sauce over the chickens and serve with the vegetables.

Boned Chicken with Parmesan

*It's really very easy to bone a whole chicken, but if you prefer,
you can ask a friendly butcher to do this for you.*

Serves 6

INGREDIENTS

1 chicken, weighing
   about 2.25 kg/5 lb
8 slices Mortadella or salami
125 g/4^1/2 oz/2 cups fresh white
   or brown breadcrumbs

125 g/4^1/2 oz/1 cup freshly
   grated Parmesan cheese
2 garlic cloves, crushed
6 tbsp chopped fresh basil
   or parsley

1 egg, beaten
pepper
fresh spring vegetables, to serve

1 Bone the chicken, keeping
the skin intact. Dislocate each
leg by breaking it at the thigh
joint. Cut down each side of the
backbone, taking care not to pierce
the breast skin.

2 Pull the backbone clear of the
flesh and discard. Remove
the ribs, severing any attached
flesh with a sharp knife.

3 Scrape the flesh from each leg
and cut away the bone at the
joint with a knife or shears.

4 Use the bones for stock. Lay
out the boned chicken on a
board, skin side down. Arrange the
Mortadella slices over the chicken,
overlapping slightly.

5 Put the breadcrumbs,
Parmesan, garlic and basil or
parsley in a bowl. Season well with
pepper and mix. Stir in the beaten
egg to bind the mixture together.
Pile the mixture down the middle
of the boned chicken, roll the meat
around it and tie securely with fine
cotton string.

6 Place in a roasting dish and
brush lightly with olive oil.
Roast in a preheated oven,
200°C/400°F/Gas Mark 6, for
1^1/2 hours or until the juices run
clear when pierced.

7 Serve hot or cold, in slices,
with fresh spring vegetables.

VARIATION

*Replace the Mortadella with rashers
of streaky bacon, if preferred.*

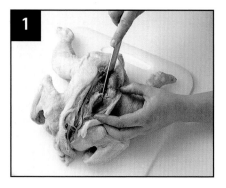
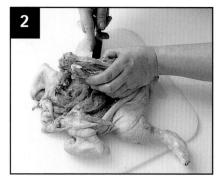
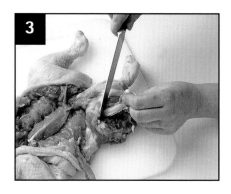

Chicken with Creamy Courgette (Zucchini) & Lime Stuffing

A cheesy stuffing is tucked under the breast skin of the chicken to give added flavour and moistness to the meat.

Serves 6

INGREDIENTS

1 chicken, weighing 2.25 kg/5 lb
oil for brushing
250 g/9 oz/1^1/3 cups courgette
   (zucchini)
25 g/1 oz/2 tbsp butter
juice of 1 lime

STUFFING:
90 g/3 oz/^{1}/2 cup courgettes
   (zucchini)
90 g/3 oz/^{3}/4 cup medium-fat
   soft cheese
finely grated rind of 1 lime

2 tbsp fresh breadcrumbs
salt and pepper

1 To make the stuffing, trim and coarsely grate the courgette (zucchini) and mix with the cheese, lime rind, breadcrumbs, salt and pepper.

2 Carefully ease the skin away from the breast of the chicken.

3 Push the stuffing under the skin with your fingers, to cover the breast evenly.

4 Place the chicken in a baking tin (pan), brush with oil and roast in a preheated oven, 190°C/ 375°F/Gas Mark 5, for 20 minutes per 500 g/1 lb 2 oz plus 20 minutes, or until the juices run clear when the thickest part of the chicken is pierced with a skewer.

5 Meanwhile, trim the remaining courgettes (zucchini) and cut into long, thin strips with a potato peeler or sharp knife. Sauté in the butter and lime juice until just tender, then serve with the chicken.

COOK'S TIP

For quicker cooking, finely grate the courgettes (zucchini) rather than cutting them into strips.

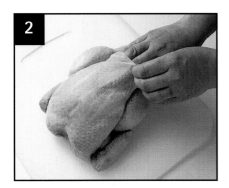

Pot Roast Orange & Sesame Chicken

This colourful, nutritious pot-roast could be served for a family meal or for a special dinner. Add more vegetables if you're feeding a crowd – if your roasting pot is large enough!

Serves 4

INGREDIENTS

2 tbsp sunflower oil
1 chicken, weighing about
   1.5 kg/3 lb 5 oz
2 large oranges
2 small onions, quartered

500 g/1 lb 2 oz/2 cups small whole
   carrots or thin carrots, cut
   into 5 cm/2 inch lengths
150 ml/¼ pint/⅔ cup orange juice
2 tbsp brandy

2 tbsp sesame seeds
1 tbsp cornflour (cornstarch)
salt and pepper

1 Heat the oil in a large flameproof casserole and fry the chicken, turning occasionally until evenly browned.

2 Cut one orange in half and place half inside the chicken cavity. Place the chicken in a large, deep casserole. Arrange the onions and carrots around the chicken.

3 Season well and pour over the orange juice.

4 Cut the remaining oranges into thin wedges and tuck around the chicken in the casserole, among the vegetables.

5 Cover and cook in a preheated oven, 180°C/350°F/ Gas Mark 4, for about 1½ hours, or until there is no trace of pink in the chicken juices when pierced, and the vegetables are tender. Remove the lid and sprinkle with the brandy and sesame seeds, and return to the oven for 10 minutes.

6 To serve, lift the chicken on to a large platter. Place the vegetables around the chicken.

Skim any excess fat from the juices. Blend the cornflour with 1 tablespoon cold water, then stir into the juices and bring to the boil, stirring all the time. Adjust the seasoning to taste, then serve the sauce with the chicken.

VARIATION

Use lemons instead of oranges for a sharper citrus flavour and place a sprig of fresh thyme in the chicken cavity with the lemon half as they are a good flavour combination.

Honey & Mustard Baked Chicken

Chicken portions are brushed with a classic combination of honey and mustard then a crunchy coating of poppy seeds is added.

Serves 4-6

INGREDIENTS

8 chicken portions
60 g/2 oz/4 tbsp butter, melted
4 tbsp mild mustard
4 tbsp clear honey
2 tbsp lemon juice
1 tsp paprika

3 tbsp poppy seeds
salt and pepper
tomato and sweetcorn salad,
   to serve

1 Place the chicken pieces, skinless side down, on a large baking tray (cookie sheet).

2 Place all the ingredients except the poppy seeds into a large bowl and blend together thoroughly.

3 Brush the mixture over the chicken portions.

4 Bake in the centre of a preheated oven, 200°C/400°F/ Gas Mark 6, for 15 minutes.

5 Carefully turn over the chicken pieces and coat the top side of the chicken with the remaining honey and mustard mixture.

6 Sprinkle the chicken with poppy seeds and return to the oven for a further 15 minutes.

7 Arrange the chicken on a serving dish, pour over the cooking juices and serve with a tomato and sweetcorn salad, if wished.

COOK'S TIP

Mexican rice makes an excellent accompaniment to this dish: boil the rice for 10 minutes, drain, then fry for 5 minutes. Add chopped onions, garlic, tomatoes, carrots and chilli and cook for 1 minute before adding stock. Bring to the boil, cover and simmer for 20 minutes, adding more stock if necessary. Add peas 5 minutes before the end of the cooking time.

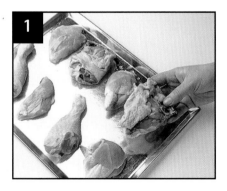

Mediterranean-style Sunday Roast

A roast that is full of Mediterranean flavour. A mixture of feta cheese, rosemary and sun-dried tomatoes is stuffed under the chicken skin, then roasted with garlic, new potatoes and vegetables.

Serves 6

INGREDIENTS

2.5 kg/5 lb 8 oz chicken
sprigs of fresh rosemary
175 g/6 oz/^{3}/$_4$ cup feta cheese,
   coarsely grated
2 tbsp sun-dried tomato paste
60 g/2 oz/4 tbsp butter, softened

1 bulb garlic
1 kg/2 lb 4 oz new potatoes, halved
   if large
1 each red, green and yellow
   (bell) pepper, cut into chunks
3 courgettes (zucchini), sliced thinly

2 tbsp olive oil
2 tbsp plain (all-purpose) flour
600 ml/1 pint/2^1/$_2$ cups chicken stock
salt and pepper

1 Rinse the chicken inside and out with cold water and drain well. Carefully cut between the skin and the top of the breast meat using a small pointed knife. Slide a finger into the slit and carefully enlarge it to form a pocket. Continue until the skin is completely lifted away from both breasts and the top of the legs.

2 Chop the leaves from 3 rosemary stems. Mix with the feta, sun-dried tomato paste, butter and pepper then spoon under the skin. Put the chicken in a large roasting tin (pan), cover with foil and cook in a preheated oven, 190°C/375°F/Gas Mark 5, for 20 minutes per 500 g/1 lb 2 oz plus 20 minutes.

3 Break the garlic bulb into cloves but do not peel. Add the vegetables to the chicken after 40 minutes.

4 Drizzle with oil, tuck in a few stems of rosemary and season well. Cook for the remaining time, removing the foil for the last 40 minutes to brown the chicken.

5 Transfer the chicken to a serving platter. Place some of the vegetables around the chicken and transfer the remainder to a warmed serving dish. Pour the fat out of the roasting tin (pan) and stir the flour into the remaining pan juices. Cook for 2 minutes then gradually stir in the stock. Bring to the boil, stirring until thickened. Strain into a sauce boat and serve with the chicken.

Cheddar Baked Chicken

Cheese and mustard, and a simple, crispy coating, make a delicious combination for this healthy dish.

Serves 4

INGREDIENTS

1 tbsp milk
2 tbsp prepared English mustard
60 g/2 oz/1 cup grated mature
  Cheddar cheese

3 tbsp plain (all-purpose) flour
2 tbsp chopped fresh chives
4 skinless, boneless chicken breasts

1 Mix together the milk and mustard in a bowl. In another bowl, combine the cheese, flour and chives.

2 Dip the chicken into the milk and mustard mixture, brushing to coat evenly.

3 Dip the chicken breasts into the cheese mixture, pressing to coat evenly. Place on a baking tray (cookie sheet) and spoon any spare cheese coating over the top.

4 Bake in a preheated oven, 200°C/400°F/Gas Mark 6, for 30–35 minutes, or until golden brown and the juices run clear, not pink, when pierced with a skewer. Serve the chicken hot, with jacket potatoes and fresh vegetables, or serve cold, with a crisp salad.

COOK'S TIP

There are several varieties of mustard available. For a sharper flavour try French varieties – Meaux mustard has a grainy texture with a warm, spicy flavour while Dijon mustard is medium-hot and tangy.

COOK'S TIP

It is a good idea to freeze herbs as they retain their colour, flavour and nutrients very well. Chives are particularly suitable for freezing – store them in labelled plastic bags and shake them dry before use. Dried chives are not an adequate substitute for fresh.

Gardener's Chicken

*Any combination of small, young vegetables can be roasted with the chicken,
such as courgettes (zucchini), leeks and onions.*

Serves 4

INGREDIENTS

250 g/9 oz/4 cups parsnips,
  peeled and chopped
125 g/4^1/2 oz/^{3}/4 cup carrots, peeled
  and chopped
25 g/1 oz/^{1}/2 cup fresh breadcrumbs
^{1}/4 tsp grated nutmeg

1 tbsp chopped fresh parsley
1.5 kg/3 lb 5 oz chicken
bunch parsley
^{1}/2 onion
25 g/1 oz/2 tbsp butter, softened
4 tbsp olive oil

500 g/1 lb 2 oz new potatoes,
  scrubbed
500 g/1 lb 2 oz baby carrots
  washed and trimmed
salt and pepper
chopped fresh parsley, to garnish

1 To make the stuffing, put the parsnips and carrots into a pan, half cover with water and bring to the boil. Cover the pan and simmer until tender. Drain well then purée in a blender or food processor. Transfer the purée to a bowl and leave to cool.

2 Mix in the breadcrumbs, nutmeg and parsley and season with salt and pepper.

3 Put the stuffing into the neck end of the chicken and push a little under the skin over the breast meat. Secure the flap of skin with a small metal skewer or cocktail stick.

4 Place the bunch of parsley and onion inside the cavity of the chicken, then place the chicken in a large roasting tin (pan).

5 Spread the butter over the skin and season with salt and pepper, cover with foil and place in a preheated oven, 190°C/375°F/Gas Mark 5, for 30 minutes.

6 Meanwhile, heat the oil in a frying pan (skillet), and lightly brown the potatoes.

7 Transfer the potatoes to the roasting tin (pan) and add the baby carrots. Baste the chicken and continue to cook for a further hour, basting the chicken and vegetables after 30 minutes. Remove the foil for the last 20 minutes to allow the skin to crisp. Garnish the vegetables with chopped parsley and serve.

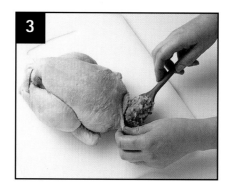

Barbecues & Grills

There is nothing more delicious than the juicy flesh and charred skin of chicken that has been grilled over an open fire – after marinating in a flavourful mixture of oil and herbs or spices. Try an Asian-style mixture of yogurt and aromatic spices, or soy sauce, sesame oil and fresh ginger root. There are some unusual flavours and innovative tastes, including Skewered Chicken with Bramble Sauce, and Skewered Chicken Spirals, which are attractive whirls of chicken, bacon and basil. Baby chickens, flavoured with lemon and tarragon in this section, are perfect for grilling (broiling) or barbecuing. There is also a recipe for Grilled (Broiled) Chicken Salad which combines chicken breasts with a selection of grilled (broiled) vegetables including courgettes, aubergine (eggplant) and red (bell) pepper drizzled with olive oil and served with crusty bread to soak up the delicious juices.

Chicken Cajun-Style

These spicy chicken wings are good served with a chilli salsa and salad. Alternatively, if this is too spicy for your taste, try a sour cream and chive dip.

Serves 4

INGREDIENTS

16 chicken wings
4 tsp paprika
2 tsp ground coriander
1 tsp celery salt
1 tsp ground cumin
$^1\!/_2$ tsp cayenne pepper

$^1\!/_2$ tsp salt
1 tbsp oil
2 tbsp red wine vinegar
fresh parsley, to garnish
cherry tomatoes and mixed salad
    leaves, to serve

1 Wash the chicken wings and pat dry with absorbent paper towels. Remove the wing tips with kitchen scissors.

2 Mix together the paprika, coriander, celery salt, cumin, cayenne pepper, salt, oil and red wine vinegar.

3 Rub this mixture over the wings to coat evenly and set aside, in the refrigerator, for at least 1 hour to allow the flavours to permeate the chicken.

4 Cook the chicken wings on a preheated barbecue (grill), occasionally brushing with oil, for about 15 minutes, turning often until cooked through. Garnish with fresh parsley and serve with cherry tomatoes, mixed salad leaves and a sauce of your choice.

COOK'S TIP

To save time, you can buy ready-made Cajun spice seasoning to rub over the chicken wings.

VARIATION

Although chicken wings do not have much meat on them, they are small and easy to pick up with your fingers which makes them ideal for barbecues (grills). However, they can also be enjoyed fried or roasted.

Spicy Sesame Chicken

*This is a quick and easy recipe for the grill, perfect
for lunch or to eat outdoors on a picnic.*

Serves 4

INGREDIENTS

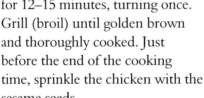

4 chicken quarters
150 g/5^1/2 oz/^{1}/2 cup
   natural (unsweetened) yogurt

finely grated rind and juice
   of 1 small lemon
2 tsp medium-hot curry paste

1 tbsp sesame seeds
lemon wedges, to serve

1 Remove the skin from the
chicken and make cuts in
the flesh at intervals with a
sharp knife.

2 In a bowl, combine the
natural (unsweetened)
yogurt, lemon rind, lemon juice
and curry paste to form a
smooth mixture.

3 Spoon the mixture over the
chicken and arrange on a foil-
lined grill (broiler) pan or baking
tray (cookie sheet).

4 Place the chicken quarters
under a preheated moderately
hot grill (broiler) and grill (broil)
for 12–15 minutes, turning once.
Grill (broil) until golden brown
and thoroughly cooked. Just
before the end of the cooking
time, sprinkle the chicken with the
sesame seeds.

5 Serve with a salad, naan bread
and lemon wedges.

COOK'S TIP

*If you have time, leave the chicken
and the sauce in the refrigerator to
marinate overnight so the flavours
are fully absorbed.*

VARIATION

*Poppy seeds, fennel seeds
or cumin seeds, or a mixture of all
three, can also be used to sprinkle
over the chicken.*

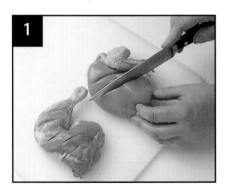

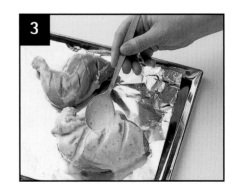

Ginger Chicken & Corn

Chicken wings and corn in a sticky ginger marinade are designed to be eaten with the fingers – there's no other way!

Serves 6

INGREDIENTS

3 cobs fresh sweetcorn
(corn-on-the-cob)
12 chicken wings

2.5cm/1 inch piece fresh ginger root
6 tbsp lemon juice
4 tsp sunflower oil

1 tbsp golden caster (superfine)
sugar

1 Remove the husks and silken hairs from the corn. Using a sharp knife, cut each cob into 6 slices. Place in a large bowl with the chicken wings.

2 Peel and grate the ginger root or chop finely.

3 Mix the ginger root with the lemon juice, sunflower oil and golden caster (superfine) sugar, then toss with the corn and chicken to coat.

4 Thread the corn and chicken wings on to skewers, to make turning easier.

5 Cook the corn and chicken under a preheated moderately hot grill (broiler) or barbecue (grill) for 15–20 minutes, basting with the gingery glaze and turning frequently until the corn is golden brown and tender and the chicken is cooked. Serve with jacket potatoes or salad.

COOK'S TIP

Cut off the wing tips before grilling (broiling) as they burn very easily. Alternatively, you can cover them with small pieces of foil.

COOK'S TIP

When you are buying fresh sweetcorn, look for plump, tightly packed kernels. If fresh corn is unavailable, you can use thawed, frozen corn instead.

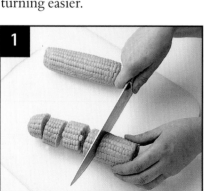

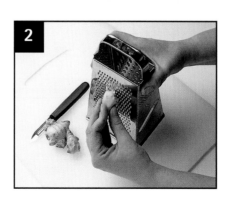

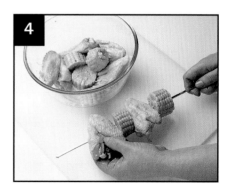

Grilled (Broiled) Chicken & Vegetable Salad

Grilling (broiling) is a quick, healthy cooking method, ideal for sealing in the juices and flavour of chicken breasts, and a wonderful way to cook summer vegetables.

Serves 4

INGREDIENTS

1 small aubergine (eggplant), sliced
2 garlic cloves, crushed
finely grated rind of $1/2$ lemon
1 tbsp chopped fresh mint
6 tbsp olive oil
4 boneless chicken breasts

2 medium courgettes (zucchini), sliced
1 medium red (bell) pepper, quartered
1 small bulb fennel, sliced thickly
1 large red onion, sliced thickly

1 small ciabatta loaf or
 1 French baguette, sliced
extra olive oil
salt and pepper

1 Place the aubergine (eggplant) slices in a colander and sprinkle with salt. Leave over a bowl to drain for 30 minutes, then rinse and dry. This will get rid of the bitter juices.

2 Mix together the garlic, lemon rind, mint, and olive oil and season.

3 Slash the chicken breasts at intervals with a sharp knife.

Spoon over about half of the oil mixture and stir to combine.

4 Combine the aubergines (eggplants) and the remaining vegetables, then toss in the remaining oil mixture. Marinate the chicken and vegetables for about 30 minutes.

5 Place the chicken breasts and vegetables on a preheated hot grill (broiler) or barbecue (grill),

turning occasionally, until they are golden brown and tender, or cook on a ridged griddle pan on the hob.

6 Brush the bread slices with olive oil and grill (broil) until golden.

7 Drizzle a little olive oil over the chicken and grilled vegetables and serve hot or cold with the crusty bread toasts.

Tropical Chicken Skewers

In this recipe, chicken is given a Caribbean flavour. The marinade keeps them moist and succulent during cooking.

Serves 6

INGREDIENTS

750 g/1 lb 10 oz boneless
  chicken breasts
2 tbsp medium sherry

3 mangoes
bay leaves
2 tbsp oil

2 tbsp coarsely shredded coconut
pepper

1 Remove the skin from the chicken and cut into 2.5 cm/1 inch cubes and toss in the sherry, with a little pepper.

2 Using a sharp knife, cut the mangoes into 2.5 cm/1 inch cubes, discarding the stone and skin.

3 Thread the chicken, mango cubes and bay leaves alternately on to long skewers, then brush lightly with oil.

4 Grill (broil) the skewers on a preheated moderately hot grill (broiler) for about 8–10 minutes, turning occasionally until golden.

5 Sprinkle the skewers with the coconut and grill (broil) for a further 30 seconds. Serve with a crisp salad.

COOK'S TIP

Use mangoes that are ripe but still firm so that they hold together on the skewers during cooking. Another firm fruit that would be suitable is pineapple.

COOK'S TIP

Remember that if you are using metal skewers, they will get very hot, so be sure to use gloves or tongs to turn them. Wooden skewers should be soaked in water for 30 minutes before use to prevent them from burning on the barbeue, and the exposed ends should be covered with pieces of kitchen foil.

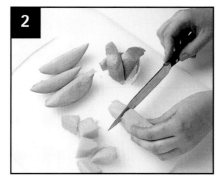

Sweet & Sour Drumsticks

Chicken drumsticks are marinated to impart a tangy, sweet and sour flavour and a shiny glaze.

Serves 4

INGREDIENTS

8 chicken drumsticks
4 tbsp red wine vinegar
2 tbsp tomato purée (paste)
2 tbsp soy sauce

2 tbsp clear honey
1 tbsp Worcestershire sauce
1 garlic clove
good pinch cayenne pepper

salt and pepper
sprig of fresh parsley, to garnish

1 Skin the chicken, if desired, and slash 2–3 times with a sharp knife.

2 Lay the chicken drumsticks side by side in a shallow non-metallic container.

3 Mix the red wine vinegar, tomato purée (paste), soy sauce, honey, Worcestershire sauce, garlic and cayenne pepper together and pour over the chicken drumsticks.

4 Leave to marinate in the refrigerator for 1 hour. Cook the drumsticks on a preheated barbecue (grill) for about 20 minutes, brushing with the marinade and turning during cooking. Garnish with parsley and serve with a crisp salad.

COOK'S TIP

For a tangy flavour, add the juice of 1 lime to the marinade. While the drumsticks are grilling, check regularly to ensure that they are not burning.

VARIATION

This sweet and sour marinade would also work well with pork or prawns (shrimp). Thread pork cubes or prawns (shrimp) on to skewers with (bell) peppers and button onions.

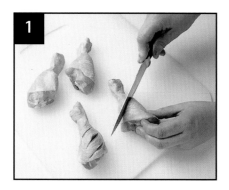

Chicken with Garden Herbs

Warm weather calls for lighter eating, and this chilled chicken dish in a subtle herb vinaigrette is ideal for a summer dinner party, or for a picnic.

Serves 4

INGREDIENTS

4 part-boned, skinless
  chicken breasts
6 tbsp olive oil
2 tbsp lemon juice

4 tbsp finely chopped summer herbs,
  such as parsley, chives and mint
1 ripe avocado

125 g/4¹/₂ oz/¹/₂ cup low-fat
  fromage frais
pepper
cold rice, to serve

---

1 Using a sharp knife, cut 3–4 deep slashes in the chicken breasts.

2 Place the chicken in a flameproof dish and brush lightly with a little of the olive oil.

3 Cook the chicken on a preheated moderately hot grill (broiler), turning once, until golden and the juices run clear when the thickest part of the chicken is pierced with a skewer.

4 Combine the remaining oil with the lemon juice and herbs and season with pepper. Spoon the oil over the chicken and leave to cool. Chill for 1 hour.

5 Remove the stone from the avocado (see Cook's Tip) and purée the flesh in a food processor with the fromage frais. Season with pepper. Serve the chicken with the avocado sauce and rice.

COOK'S TIP

The chicken can be cooked several hours in advance and stored in the refrigerator until required.

COOK'S TIP

To remove the stone easily from an avocado, first cut the avocado in half. Holding one half securely in your hand, tap the knife into the stone so that it becomes embedded, then carefully twist the knife to dislodge the stone.

Skewered Spicy Tomato Chicken

These low-fat, spicy skewers are cooked in a matter of minutes. In addition, they can be assembled ahead of time and stored in the refrigerator until you need them.

Serves 4

INGREDIENTS

500 g/1 lb 2 oz skinless, boneless
   chicken breasts
3 tbsp tomato purée (paste)
2 tbsp clear honey

2 tbsp Worcestershire sauce
1 tbsp chopped fresh rosemary
250 g/9 oz cherry tomatoes
sprigs of rosemary, to garnish

couscous or rice, to serve

1 Using a sharp knife, cut the chicken into 2.5 cm/1 inch chunks and place in a bowl.

2 Mix together the tomato purée (paste), honey, Worcestershire sauce and rosemary. Add to the chicken, stirring to coat evenly.

3 Alternating the chicken pieces and tomatoes, thread them on to eight wooden skewers. Spoon over any remaining glaze.

4 Cook under a preheated hot grill (broiler) for 8–10 minutes, turning occasionally, until the chicken is thoroughly cooked. Serve on a bed of couscous or rice and garnish with sprigs of rosemary.

COOK'S TIP

Couscous is made from semolina that has been made into separate grains. It is very easy to prepare – simply soak it in a bowl of boiling water and then fluff up the grains with a fork. Flavourings such as lemon or nutmeg can be added.

COOK'S TIP

Cherry tomatoes are ideal for barbecues as they can be threaded straight on to skewers. As they are kept whole, the skins keep in the tomatoes natural juices.

Grilled (Broiled) Chicken with Pesto Toasts

This Italian-style dish is richly flavoured with pesto, which is a mixture of basil, olive oil, pine nuts and Parmesan cheese. Either red or green pesto can be used for this recipe.

Serves 4

INGREDIENTS

8 part-boned chicken thighs
olive oil, for brushing
400 ml/14 fl oz/1²/₃ cups
   passata (sieved tomatoes)

120 ml/4 fl oz/¹/₂ cup green
   or red pesto sauce
12 slices French bread
90 g/3 oz/1 cup freshly grated
   Parmesan cheese

60 g/2 oz/¹/₂ cup pine nuts
   or flaked (slivered) almonds
salad leaves, to serve

1 Arrange the chicken in a single layer in a wide flameproof dish and brush lightly with oil. Place under a preheated grill (broiler) for about 15 minutes, turning occasionally, until golden brown.

2 Pierce the chicken with a skewer to ensure that there is no trace of pink in the juices.

3 Pour off any excess fat. Warm the passata (sieved tomatoes) and half the pesto sauce in a small pan and pour over the chicken. Grill (broil) for a few more minutes, turning until coated.

4 Meanwhile, spread the remaining pesto on to the slices of bread. Arrange the bread over the chicken and sprinkle with the Parmesan cheese. Scatter the pine nuts over the cheese. Grill (broil) for 2–3 minutes, or until browned and bubbling. Serve with a selection of salad leaves.

COOK'S TIP

Although leaving the skin on the chicken means that it will have a higher fat content, many people like the rich taste and crispy skin especially when it is blackened by the barbecue (grill). The skin also keeps in the cooking juices.

Mustardy Barbecue Drummers

*Great for barbecues (grills), or for simple summer lunches and picnics,
this is an easy and tasty recipe for chicken drumsticks.*

Serves 4

INGREDIENTS

10 slices smoked streaky bacon
1 garlic clove, peeled
   and crushed
3 tbsp wholegrain mustard

4 tbsp fresh brown breadcrumbs
8 chicken drumsticks

1 tbsp sunflower oil
fresh parsley sprigs, to garnish

1 Chop two of the bacon slices into small pieces and fry without fat for 3–4 minutes, stirring so that the bacon does not stick to the bottom of the pan. Remove from the heat and stir in the crushed garlic, 2 tablespoons of wholegrain mustard and the breadcrumbs.

2 Carefully loosen the skin from each drumstick with your fingers, being careful not to tear the skin. Spoon a little of the mustard stuffing under each flap of skin, smoothing the skins over firmly afterwards.

3 Wrap a bacon rasher around each drumstick, and secure with cocktail sticks (toothpicks).

4 Mix together the remaining mustard and the oil, brush over the chicken drumsticks and cook on a preheated moderately hot barbecue or grill (broiler) for about 25 minutes, until there is no trace of pink in the juices when the thickest part of the chicken is pierced with a skewer.

5 Garnish with the parsley sprigs. The drumsticks may be served hot or cold.

COOK'S TIP

Don't cook the chicken over the hottest part of the barbecue (grill) or the outside may be charred before the centre is cooked.

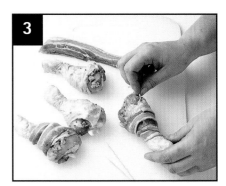

Minty Lime Chicken

These tangy lime and honey-coated pieces have a matching sauce or dip based on creamy natural (unsweetened) yogurt. They could be served at a barbecue or as a main course for a dinner party.

Serves 6

INGREDIENTS

3 tbsp finely chopped mint
4 tbsp clear honey
4 tbsp lime juice
12 boneless chicken thighs

SAUCE:
150 g/5^1/$_2$ oz/^{1}/$_2$ cup natural
   (unsweetened) thick yogurt
1 tbsp finely chopped mint
2 tsp finely grated lime rind

1 Combine the mint, honey and lime juice in a bowl.

2 Use cocktail sticks to keep the chicken thighs in neat shapes and add the chicken to the marinade, turning to coat evenly.

3 Leave to marinate for at least 30 minutes, preferably overnight. Cook the chicken on a preheated moderately hot barbecue (grill) or grill (broiler), turning frequently and basting with the marinade. The chicken is cooked if the juices run clear when the chicken is pierced in the thickest part with a skewer.

4 Meanwhile, mix together the sauce ingredients.

5 Remove the cocktail sticks and serve the chicken with a salad and the sauce.

VARIATION

Use this marinade for chicken kebabs, alternating the chicken with lime and red onion wedges.

COOK'S TIP

Mint can be grown very easily in a garden or window box. It is a useful herb for marinades and salad dressings. Other useful herbs to grow are parsley and basil.

Skewered Chicken with Bramble Sauce

*This autumnal recipe can be made with fresh-picked wild blackberries
from the hedgerow if you're lucky enough to have a good supply.*

Serves 4

INGREDIENTS

4 chicken breasts or 8 thighs
4 tbsp dry white wine or cider
2 tbsp chopped fresh rosemary
pepper

rosemary sprigs
  and blackberries, to garnish
green salad, to serve

SAUCE:
200 g/7 oz/scant 2 cups blackberries
1 tbsp cider vinegar
2 tbsp redcurrant jelly
$1/4$ tsp grated nutmeg

1 Using a sharp knife, cut the chicken into 2.5cm/1 inch pieces and place in a bowl. Sprinkle over the white wine and rosemary, and season well with pepper. Cover and leave to marinate for at least an hour.

2 Drain the chicken, reserving the marinade, and thread the meat on to 8 metal or pre-soaked wooden skewers.

3 Cook on a preheated moderately hot grill (broiler) for 8–10 minutes, turning occasionally, until golden and evenly cooked.

4 Meanwhile, to make the sauce, place the marinade in a pan with the blackberries and simmer gently until soft. Press the mixture though a sieve (strainer) using the back of a spoon.

5 Return the blackberry purée to the pan with the cider vinegar and redcurrant jelly and bring to the boil. Boil uncovered until the sauce is reduced by about one-third.

6 Spoon a little bramble sauce on to each plate and place a chicken skewer on top. Sprinkle with nutmeg and serve hot. Garnish with rosemary and blackberries and serve.

COOK'S TIP

*If you use canned fruit,
omit the redcurrant jelly.*

Grilled (Broiled) Poussin with Lemon & Tarragon

Spatchcocked baby chickens are complemented by the delicate fragrance of lemon and tarragon and grilled (broiled).

Serves 2

INGREDIENTS

2 baby chickens
4 sprigs fresh tarragon
1 tsp oil
25 g/1 oz/2 tbsp butter

rind of 1/2 lemon
1 tbsp lemon juice
1 garlic clove, crushed
salt and pepper

tarragon and orange slices,
to garnish

1 Prepare the baby chickens, turn them breast-side down on a chopping board and cut them through the backbone using kitchen scissors. Crush each bird gently to break the bones so that they lie flat while cooking. Season each with salt.

2 Turn them over and insert a sprig of tarragon under the skin over each side of the breast.

3 Brush the chickens with oil, using a pastry brush, and place under a preheated hot grill (broiler) about 13 cm/5 inches from the heat. Grill (broil) the chickens for about 15 minutes, turning half way, until they are lightly browned.

4 Meanwhile, to make the glaze, melt the butter in a small saucepan, add the lemon rind, lemon juice and garlic and season with salt and pepper.

5 Brush the baby chickens with the glaze and cook for a further 15 minutes, turning them once and brushing regularly so that they stay moist. Garnish the chickens with tarragon and orange slices and serve with new potatoes.

COOK'S TIP

Once the chickens are flattened, insert 2 metal skewers through them to keep them flat.

Barbecued (Grilled) Chicken Quarters with Warm Aioli

Chicken quarters are barbecued (grilled) then served with a strongly flavoured garlic mayonnaise, which originated in Provence, France.

Serves 4

INGREDIENTS

4 chicken quarters
2 tbsp oil
2 tbsp lemon juice
2 tsp dried thyme
salt and pepper

green salad and lemon slices, to serve

AIOLI:
5 garlic cloves, crushed
2 egg yolks

120 ml/4 fl oz/$^1/_2$ cup each olive oil and sunflower oil
2 tsp lemon juice
2 tbsp boiling water

1 Using a skewer, prick the chicken quarters in several places then place them in a shallow dish.

2 Combine the oil, lemon juice, thyme and seasoning, then pour over the chicken, turning to coat the chicken evenly. Set aside for 2 hours.

3 To make the aioli, beat together the garlic and a pinch of salt to make a paste. Add the egg yolks and beat well.

Gradually add the oils, drop by drop, beating vigorously, until the mayonnaise becomes creamy and smooth. Add the oils in a thin steady trickle and continue beating until the aioli is thick. Stir in the lemon juice and season with pepper. Set aside in a warm place.

4 Place the chicken on a preheated barbecue (grill) and cook for 25–30 minutes. Brush with the marinade and turn the portions to cook evenly. Remove and arrange on a serving plate.

5 Beat the water into the aioli and turn into a warmed serving bowl. Serve the chicken with the aioli, a green salad and lemon slices.

COOK'S TIP

To make a quick aioli, add the garlic to 300 ml/$^1/_2$ pint/1$^1/_4$ cups good quality mayonnaise then place in a bowl over a pan of warm water and beat together. Just before serving add 1–2 tbsp hot water.

Skewered Chicken Spirals

These unusual chicken kebabs (kabobs) have a wonderful Mediterranean flavour, and the bacon helps keep them moist during cooking.

Serves 4

INGREDIENTS

4 skinless, boneless chicken breasts
1 garlic clove, crushed
2 tbsp tomato purée (paste)

4 slices smoked back bacon
large handful fresh basil leaves
oil for brushing

salt and pepper

1 Spread out a piece of chicken between two sheets of cling film (plastic wrap) and beat firmly with a rolling pin to flatten the chicken to an even thickness. Repeat with the remaining pieces of chicken.

2 Mix together the crushed garlic and tomato purée (paste) until well blended. Spread the mixture evenly over the surface of the chicken.

3 Lay a bacon slice over each piece of chicken, then scatter with the fresh basil leaves. Season well with salt and pepper.

4 Roll up each piece of chicken firmly, then cut into thick slices using a sharp knife.

5 Thread the slices securely on to four skewers, making sure the skewer holds the chicken in a spiral shape.

6 Brush the skewers lightly with oil and cook on a preheated hot barbecue (grill) or grill (broiler) for about 5 minutes, then turn the skewers over and cook for a further 5 minutes, until the chicken is cooked through. Serve the chicken spirals hot with a green salad.

COOK'S TIP

Flattening the chicken breasts makes them thinner so that they cook more quickly. It also makes them easier to roll.

VARIATION

To complete the Mediterranean theme, serve these kebabs (kabobs) with Parmesan-topped garlic bread.

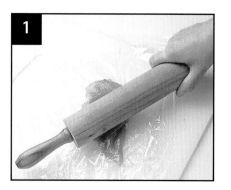
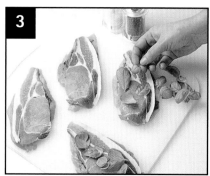
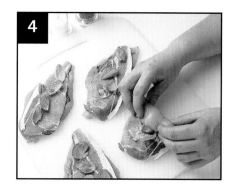

Spicy Dishes

Because chicken is popular throughout the world, there are countless spicy recipes from Asia, Mexico, the Caribbean, Spain and Japan. Lime juice, peanut, coconut and chilli add the authentic tastes of Thailand to Chilli Coconut Chicken, while Kashmiri Chicken is a rich and spicy dish from Northern India with an aromatic sauce made from yogurt, Tikka curry paste, cumin, ginger, chilli and almonds. From Spain comes Spanish Chicken with Prawns with its unusual mixture of chicken and shellfish, together with the famous spicy Spanish sausage, chorizo, slow-cooked in a sauce of garlic, tomatoes and white wine. Cumin Spiced Apricot Chicken is a creative modern dish that would be perfect for any special occasion. The chicken is stuffed with dried apricots, coated in a yogurt, cumin and turmeric sauce and served with nutty rice. There is even a dish from Japan, Teppanyaki, a simple dish of fried chicken slices with (bell) peppers, spring onions (scallions) and bean sprouts, served with a Mirin dipping sauce.

Chicken in Red (Bell) Pepper & Almond Sauce

This tasty chicken dish combines warm spices and almonds and is spiked with anise.

Serves 4

INGREDIENTS

25 g/1 oz/2 tbsp butter
7 tbsp vegetable oil
4 skinless, boneless chicken
   breasts, cut into 4 cm/2 inch
   x 2 cm/1 inch pieces
1 medium onion, roughly chopped
2 cm/1 inch piece fresh ginger root
3 garlic cloves, peeled

25 g/1 oz/^{1}/$_4$ cup blanched almonds
1 large red (bell) pepper,
   roughly chopped
1 tbsp ground cumin
2 tsp ground coriander
1 tsp ground turmeric
pinch cayenne pepper
^{1}/$_2$ tsp salt

150 ml/^{1}/$_4$ pint/^{2}/$_3$ cup water
3 star anise
2 tbsp lemon juice
pepper
flaked (slivered) almonds,
   to garnish
rice, to serve

1 Heat the butter and 1 tablespoon of oil in a frying pan (skillet), add the chicken pieces and cook for 5 minutes until golden. Transfer the chicken pieces to a plate and keep warm until required.

2 Combine the onion, ginger, garlic, almonds, red (bell) pepper, cumin, coriander, turmeric, cayenne pepper and salt in a food processor or liquidiser. Blend to form a smooth paste.

3 Heat the remaining oil in a large saucepan or deep frying pan (skillet). Add the paste and fry for 10–12 minutes.

4 Add the chicken pieces, the water, star anise, lemon juice and pepper. Cover, reduce the heat and simmer gently for 25 minutes or until the chicken is tender, stirring a few times during cooking.

5 Transfer the chicken to a serving dish, sprinkle with the flaked (slivered) almonds and serve with individual rice moulds.

Fruity Garlic Curried Chicken

Serve this fruity curry with mango chutney and naan bread, and top the curry with seedless grapes. Mangoes or pears make a good substitute for pineapple.

Serves 4-6

INGREDIENTS

1 tbsp oil
900 g/2 lb chicken meat, chopped
60 g/2 oz/4 tbsp flour, seasoned
32 shallots, roughly chopped
4 garlic cloves,
   crushed with a little olive oil
3 cooking apples, diced

1 pineapple, diced
125 g/4^1/$_2$ oz/^{3}/$_4$ cup sultanas
   (golden raisins)
1 tbsp clear honey
300 ml/^{1}/$_2$ pint/1^1/$_4$ cups chicken
   stock
2 tbsp Worcestershire sauce

3 tbsp hot curry paste
150 ml/^{1}/$_4$ pint/^{2}/$_3$ cup soured cream
salt and pepper
orange slices, to garnish
rice, to serve

1 Heat the oil in a large frying pan (skillet). Coat the meat in the seasoned flour and cook for about 4 minutes until it is browned all over. Transfer the chicken to a large deep casserole and keep warm until required.

2 Slowly fry the shallots, garlic, apples, pineapple and sultanas (golden raisins) in the pan juices.

3 Add the honey, chicken stock, Worcestershire sauce and hot curry paste. Season to taste with salt and pepper.

4 Pour the sauce over the chicken and cover the casserole with a lid or cooking foil.

5 Cook in the centre of a preheated oven, 180°C/350°F/ Gas Mark 4, for about 2 hours. Stir in the soured cream and cook for a further 15 minutes. Serve the curry with rice, garnished with a slice of orange.

VARIATION

Coconut rice also makes an excellent accompaniment to this dish. Place 25 g/1 oz chopped creamed coconut, 1 cinnamon stick, 600 ml/1 pint/2^1/$_4$ cups water in a large saucepan and bring to the boil. Stir in 350 g/12 oz/1^3/$_4$ cups basmati rice, cover and simmer gently for 15 minutes until all the liquid has been absorbed. Remove the cinnamon stick before serving.

Spicy Chicken Tortillas

Serve these easy-to-prepare tortillas to friends or as a special family supper.
The chicken filling has a mild, mellow spicy heat and a fresh salad makes a perfect accompaniment.

Serves 4

INGREDIENTS

2 tbsp oil
8 skinless, boneless chicken
  thighs, sliced
1 onion, chopped
2 garlic cloves, chopped
1 tsp cumin seeds, roughly crushed
2 large dried chillies, sliced

400 g/14 oz can tomatoes
400 g/14 oz can red kidney
  beans, drained
150 ml/^{1}/$_4$ pint/^{2}/$_3$ cup chicken stock
2 tsp sugar
salt and pepper
lime wedges, to garnish

TO SERVE:
1 large ripe avocado
1 lime
8 soft tortillas
250 ml/9 fl oz/1 cup thick yogurt

1 Heat the oil in a large frying pan (skillet) or wok, add the chicken and fry for 3 minutes until golden. Add the onion and fry for 5 minutes, stirring until browned. Add the garlic, cumin and chillies, with their seeds, and cook for about 1 minute.

2 Add the tomatoes, kidney beans, stock, sugar and salt and pepper to taste. Bring to the boil, breaking up the tomatoes. Cover and simmer for 15 minutes.

Remove the lid and cook for 5 minutes, stirring occasionally until the sauce has thickened.

3 Halve the avocado, discard the stone and scoop out the flesh on to a plate. Mash the avocado with a fork. Cut half of the lime into 8 thin wedges. Squeeze the juice from the remaining lime over the avocado.

4 Warm the tortillas following the instructions on the packet.

Put two tortillas on each serving plate, fill with the chicken mixture and top with spoonfuls of avocado and yogurt. Garnish the tortillas with lime wedges.

VARIATION

For a vegetarian filling, replace the chicken with 400 g/14 oz canned pinto or cannellini beans and use vegetable stock instead of the chicken stock.

Cajun Chicken Gumbo

This complete main course is cooked in one saucepan for simplicity. If you're cooking for one, simply halve the ingredients; the cooking time should stay the same.

Serves 2

INGREDIENTS

1 tbsp sunflower oil
4 chicken thighs
1 small onion, diced
2 sticks (stalks) celery, diced

1 small green (bell) pepper, diced
90 g/3 oz/$^1/_2$ cup long grain rice
300 ml/$^1/_2$ pint/1$^1/_4$ cups
   chicken stock

1 small red chilli
250 g/9 oz okra
15 ml/1 tbsp tomato purée (paste)
salt and pepper

1 Heat the oil in a wide pan and fry the chicken until golden. Remove the chicken from the pan using a slotted spoon. Stir in the onion, celery and (bell) pepper and fry for 1 minute. Pour off any excess fat.

2 Add the rice and fry, stirring briskly, for a further minute. Add the chicken stock and heat until boiling.

3 Thinly slice the chilli and trim the okra. Add to the pan with the tomato purée (paste). Season to taste.

4 Return the chicken to the pan and stir. Cover tightly and simmer gently for 15 minutes, or until the rice is tender, the chicken is thoroughly cooked and all the liquid absorbed. Stir occasionally and if the gumbo becomes too dry, add a little extra stock to moisten. Serve immediately.

COOK'S TIP

The whole chilli makes the dish hot and spicy – if you prefer a milder flavour, discard the seeds of the chilli.

VARIATION

You can replace the chicken with 250 g/9 oz peeled prawns (shrimp) and 90 g/3 oz belly of pork, if desired. Slice the pork and fry in the oil before adding the onions, and add the prawns (shrimp) 5 minutes before the end of cooking time.

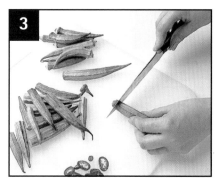

Mexican Chicken

*Chilli, tomatoes and corn are typical ingredients
in a Mexican dish.*

Serves 4

INGREDIENTS

2 tbsp oil
8 chicken drumsticks
1 medium onion, finely chopped
1 tsp chilli powder

1 tsp ground coriander
400 g/14 oz can chopped tomatoes
2 tbsp tomato purée (paste)
125 g/4$^{1}/_{2}$ oz/$^{2}/_{3}$ cup frozen
   sweetcorn (corn-on-the-cob)

salt and pepper
rice and mixed (bell) pepper salad,
   to serve

1 Heat the oil in a large frying pan (skillet), add the chicken drumsticks and cook over a medium heat until lightly browned. Remove the chicken drumsticks from the pan with a slotted spoon and set aside until required.

2 Add the chopped onion to the pan and cook for 3–4 minutes until softened, then stir in the chilli powder and coriander and cook for a few seconds, stirring briskly so the spices do not burn on the bottom of the pan. Add the chopped tomatoes with their juice and the tomato purée (paste) and stir well to incorporate.

3 Return the chicken drumsticks to the pan and simmer the casserole gently for 20 minutes until the chicken is tender and thoroughly cooked. Add the sweetcorn (corn-on-the-cob) and cook for a further 3–4 minutes. Season with salt and pepper to taste.

4 Serve the Mexican Chicken with rice and mixed (bell) pepper salad.

COOK'S TIP

Mexican dishes are not usually suitable for freezing because the strong flavours they contain, such as chilli, intensify during freezing, and if left for too long, an unpleasant, musty flavour can develop.

Chicken with (Bell) Peppers & Black Bean Sauce

This tasty chicken stir-fry is quick and easy to make and is full of fresh flavours and crunchy vegetables.

Serves 4

INGREDIENTS

400 g/14 oz chicken breasts, sliced thinly
pinch of cornflour (cornstarch)
2 tbsp oil
1 garlic clove, crushed
1 tbsp black bean sauce
1 each small red and green (bell) pepper, cut into strips

1 red chilli, chopped finely
75 g/2^3/4 oz/1 cup mushrooms, sliced
1 onion, chopped
6 spring onions (scallions), chopped
salt and pepper
fresh noodles, to serve

SEASONING:
^{1}/2 tsp salt
^{1}/2 tsp sugar
3 tbsp chicken stock
1 tbsp dark soy sauce
2 tbsp beef stock
2 tbsp rice wine
1 tsp cornflour (cornstarch), blended with a little rice wine

1 Put the chicken strips in a bowl. Add a pinch of salt and a pinch of cornflour and cover with water. Leave for 30 minutes.

2 Heat 1 tbsp of the oil in a wok or deep-sided frying pan (skillet) and stir-fry the chicken for 4 minutes. Transfer the chicken to a warm serving dish and clean the wok or pan.

3 Add the remaining oil to the wok and add the garlic, black bean sauce, green and red (bell) peppers, chilli, mushrooms, onion and spring onions (scallions). Stir-fry the vegetables for 2 minutes then return the chicken strips to the wok.

4 Add the seasoning ingredients, fry for 3 minutes and thicken with a little of the cornflour (cornstarch) paste. Serve with fresh noodles.

COOK'S TIP

Black bean sauce can be found in specialist shops and in many supermarkets. Use dried noodles if you can't find fresh noodles.

Teppanyaki

This simple, Japanese style of cooking is ideal for thinly sliced breast of chicken. Mirin is a rich, sweet rice wine which is available from oriental shops.

Serves 4

INGREDIENTS

4 boneless chicken breasts
1 red (bell) pepper
1 green (bell) pepper
4 spring onions (scallions)

8 baby corn cobs (corn-on-the-cob)
100g/3^1/$_2$ oz/^{1}/$_2$ cup bean sprouts
1 tbsp sesame or sunflower oil
4 tbsp soy sauce

4 tbsp mirin
1 tbsp grated fresh ginger root

1 Remove the skin from the chicken and slice at a slight angle, to a thickness of about 5 mm/¼ inch.

2 Deseed and thinly slice the (bell) peppers and trim and slice the spring onions (scallions) and corn cobs (corn-on-the-cob). Arrange the (bell) peppers, spring onions (scallions), corn cobs and bean sprouts on a plate with the sliced chicken.

3 Heat a large griddle or heavy frying pan (skillet) then lightly brush with oil. Add the vegetables and chicken slices in small batches, allowing space between them so that they cook thoroughly.

4 In a small bowl, mix together the soy sauce, mirin and ginger and serve as a dip with the chicken and vegetables.

VARIATION

If you cannot find mirin, add one tablespoon of soft, light brown sugar to the sauce instead.

VARIATION

Instead of serving the sauce as a dip, you could use it as a marinade. However, do not leave it to marinate for more than 2 hours as the soy sauce will cause the chicken to dry out and become tough. Use other vegetables, such as mangetout (snow peas) or thinly sliced carrots, if you prefer.

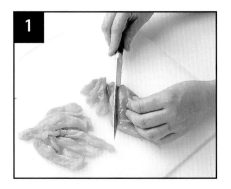

Caribbean Chicken

This exotic dish can be made with any cut of chicken, but drumsticks are best for quick and even cooking. Grated fresh coconut adds a delicious, tropical flavour.

Serves 4

INGREDIENTS

8 skinless chicken drumsticks
2 limes
1 tsp cayenne pepper
2 medium mangoes

1 tbsp sunflower oil
2 tbsp dark muscovado sugar
lime wedges and fresh parsley,
  to garnish

2 tbsp coarsely grated coconut
  (optional), to serve

1 With a sharp knife, slash the chicken drumsticks at intervals then place the chicken in a large bowl.

2 Grate the rind from the limes and set aside.

3 Squeeze the juice from the limes and sprinkle over the chicken with the cayenne pepper. Cover and chill in the refrigerator for at least two hours or overnight.

4 Peel the mangoes and chop in half. Discard the stone and cut the flesh into slices.

5 Drain the chicken drumsticks using a slotted spoon and reserve the juice. Heat the oil in a wide heavy pan and sauté the chicken drumsticks, turning frequently, until golden. Stir in the marinade, lime rind, mango slices and the dark muscovado sugar.

6 Cover the pan and simmer gently, stirring occasionally, for 15 minutes, or until the chicken juices run clear when pierced with a skewer. Sprinkle with grated coconut, if using, and garnish with lime wedges and fresh parsley.

VARIATION

When buying mangoes, bear in mind that the skin of ripe mangoes varies in colour from green to pinky-red and the flesh from pale yellow to bright orange. Choose mangoes which yield to gentle pressure.

Spanish Chicken with Prawns (Shrimps)

This unusual dish, with its mixture of chicken and shellfish, is typically Spanish. The basis of this recipe is sofrito: a slow-cooked mixture of onion and tomato in olive oil, with garlic and peppers.

Serves 4

INGREDIENTS

4 chicken quarters
1 tbsp olive oil
1 red (bell) pepper
1 medium onion
2 garlic cloves, crushed

400 g/14 oz can chopped tomatoes
200 ml/7 fl oz/scant 1 cup
  dry white wine
4 tbsp chopped fresh oregano
125 g/4^1/2 oz/1 cup chorizo sausage

125 g/4^1/2 oz/1 cup peeled
  prawns (shrimp)
salt and pepper
rice, to serve

1 Remove the skin from the chicken quarters. Heat the oil in a wide, heavy pan and fry the chicken, turning occasionally until golden brown.

2 Using a sharp knife, deseed and slice the (bell) pepper and peel and slice the onion. Add the (bell) pepper and onion to the pan and fry gently to soften.

3 Add the garlic with the tomatoes, wine and oregano.

Season well with salt and pepper, then bring to the boil, cover and simmer gently for 45 minutes or until the chicken is tender and the juices run clear when the thickest part of the chicken is pierced with a skewer.

4 Thinly slice the chorizo and add to the pan together with the prawns (shrimp), then simmer for a further 5 minutes. Adjust the seasoning to taste and serve with rice.

COOK'S TIP

Chorizo is a spicy Spanish sausage made with pork and a hot pepper such as cayenne or pimento. It is available from large supermarkets and specialist butchers.

Chicken Korma

Korma is a typically mild and aromatic curry. If you want to reduce the fat in this recipe, use natural (unsweetened) yogurt instead of the cream.

Serves 4-6

INGREDIENTS

750 g/1 lb 10 oz chicken meat,
   cut into cubes
300 ml/¹/₂ pint/1¹/₄ cups double
   (heavy) cream
¹/₂ tsp garam masala

KORMA PASTE:
2 garlic cloves
2.5 cm/1 inch fresh ginger root,
   coarsely chopped
50 g/1³/₄ oz/¹/₃ cup blanched
   almonds
6 tbsp chicken stock
1 tsp ground cardomon
4 cloves, crushed

1 tsp cinnamon
2 large onions, chopped
1 tsp coriander seeds
2 tsp ground cumin seeds
pinch cayenne
6 tbsp olive oil
salt and pepper
coriander (cilantro), to garnish

1 Place all the ingredients for the korma paste into a blender or food processor and blend together until a very smooth paste is formed.

2 Place the cubes of chicken in a bowl and pour over the korma paste. Stir to coat the chicken completely with the paste. Cover and chill in the refrigerator for 3 hours to allow the flavours to permeate the chicken.

3 Simmer the meat in a large saucepan for 25 minutes, adding a little chicken stock if the mixture becomes too dry.

4 Add the double (heavy) cream and garam masala to the pan and simmer for a further 15 minutes. Allow the korma to stand for 10 minutes before serving. Garnish the chicken korma with fresh coriander (cilantro) and serve with rice.

COOK'S TIP

Garam masala is the name given to the mixture of spices commonly used as a base in curries. It can be bought ready-mixed or you can prepare your own by grinding together 1 tsp cardamon seeds, 2 tsp cloves, 2 tbsp each cumin seeds and coriander seeds, 7.5 cm/3 inch piece cinnamon stick, 1 tbsp black peppercorns and 1 dried red chilli.

Regal Chicken with Cashew Nut Stuffing

Most of the flavourful stuffing is cooked separately from the chicken, only a small amount is added to the neck end.

Serves 4

INGREDIENTS

1 chicken, weighing about
   1.5 kg/3 lb 5 oz
1 small onion, halved
25 g/1 oz/2 tbsp butter, melted
1 tsp ground turmeric
1 tsp ground ginger
$^1/_2$ tsp cayenne
salt and pepper
fresh coriander (cilantro), to garnish

STUFFING:
2 tbsp oil
1 medium onion, chopped finely
$^1/_2$ medium red (bell) pepper,
   chopped finely
2 garlic cloves, crushed
125 g/4$^1/_2$ oz/$^1/_2$ cup basmati rice
350 ml/12 fl oz/1$^1/_2$ cups
   hot chicken stock

grated rind of $^1/_2$ lemon
$^1/_2$ tsp ground turmeric
$^1/_2$ tsp ground ginger
$^1/_2$ tsp ground coriander
pinch cayenne pepper
90 g/3 oz/$^1/_2$ cup salted cashew
   nuts

1 To make the stuffing, heat the oil in a saucepan, add the onion, red (bell) pepper and garlic and cook gently for 4–5 minutes. Add the rice and stir to coat in the oil. Add the stock, bring to the boil, then simmer for 15 minutes until all the liquid is absorbed. Transfer to a bowl and add the remaining ingredients for the stuffing. Season well with pepper.

2 Place half the stuffing in the neck end of the chicken and secure with a cocktail stick. Put the halved onion into the cavity of the chicken. Spoon the rest of the rice stuffing into a greased ovenproof dish and cover with foil.

3 Place the chicken in a roasting tin (pan). Prick all over avoiding the stuffed area. Mix the butter and spices, season, then brush over the chicken.

4 Roast in a preheated oven, 190°C/375°F/Gas Mark 5, for 1 hour, basting from time to time. Place the dish of rice stuffing in the oven and continue cooking the chicken for 30 minutes. Remove the cocktail stick and serve the chicken with stuffing and gravy.

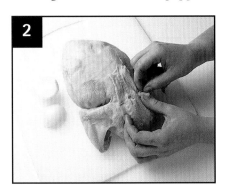

Thai Stir-Fried Chicken with Vegetables

Coconut adds a creamy texture and delicious flavour to this Thai-style stir-fry, which is spiked with green chilli.

Serves 4

INGREDIENTS

3 tbsp sesame oil
350 g/12 oz chicken breast,
　sliced thinly
8 shallots, sliced
2 garlic cloves, finely chopped
2.5 cm/1 inch piece fresh
　root ginger, grated

1 green chilli, finely chopped
1 each red and green (bell) pepper,
　sliced thinly
3 courgettes (zucchini),
　thinly sliced
2 tbsp ground almonds
1 tsp ground cinnamon

1 tbsp oyster sauce
50 g/1^3/$_4$ oz/^{1}/$_4$ cup creamed
　coconut, grated
salt and pepper

1 Heat the sesame oil in a wok, add the chicken, season with salt and pepper, and stir fry for about 4 minutes.

2 Add the shallots, garlic, ginger and chilli and stir-fry for 2 minutes.

3 Add the (bell) peppers and courgettes (zucchini) and cook for about 1 minute.

4 Finally, add the remaining ingredients and seasoning. Stir-fry for 1 minute and serve.

COOK'S TIP

Creamed coconut is sold in blocks by supermarkets and oriental stores. It is a useful store-cupboard standby as it adds richness and depth of flavour.

COOK'S TIP

Since most of the heat of chillies comes from the seeds, remove them before cooking if you want a milder flavour. Be very careful when handling chillies – do not touch your face or eyes as the chilli juice can be very painful. Always wash your hands after preparing chillies.

Golden Chicken Pilau

This is a simple version of a creamy textured and mildly spiced Indian pilau. Although there are lots of ingredients, there's very little preparation needed for this dish.

Serves 4

INGREDIENTS

60 g/2 oz/4 tbsp butter
8 skinless, boneless chicken thighs,
  cut into large pieces
1 medium onion, sliced
1 tsp ground turmeric
1 tsp ground cinnamon
250 g/9 oz/1 cup long
  grain rice

425 ml/^{3}/$_4$ pint/1^3/$_4$ cups
  natural (unsweetened) yogurt
60 g/2 oz/^{1}/$_3$ cup sultanas (golden
  raisins)
200 ml/7 fl oz/1 scant cup chicken
  stock
1 medium tomato, chopped

2 tbsp chopped fresh coriander
  (cilantro) or parsley
2 tbsp toasted coconut
salt and pepper
fresh coriander (cilantro),
  to garnish

1 Heat the butter in a heavy or non-stick pan and fry the chicken with the onion for about 3 minutes.

2 Stir in the turmeric, cinnamon, rice and seasoning and fry gently for 3 minutes.

3 Add the natural (unsweetened) yogurt, sultanas (golden raisins) and chicken stock and mix well. Cover and simmer for 10 minutes, stirring occasionally until the rice is tender and all the stock has been absorbed. Add more stock if the mixture becomes too dry.

4 Stir in the chopped tomato and fresh coriander (cilantro) or parsley.

5 Sprinkle the pilau with the toasted coconut and garnish with fresh coriander (cilantro).

COOK'S TIP

Long-grain rice is the most widely available and the cheapest rice. Basmati, with its slender grains and aromatic flavour is more expensive and should be used on special occasions if it is not affordable on a frequent basis. Rice, especially basmati, should be washed thoroughly under cold, running water before use.

Kashmiri Chicken

This warming, rich and spicy dish is based on the traditional cooking style of Northern India, using chicken on the bone.

Serves 4

INGREDIENTS

4 skinless chicken drumsticks
4 skinless chicken thighs
150 ml/^{1}/$_4$ pint/^{2}/$_3$ cup
    natural (unsweetened) yogurt
4 tbsp Tikka curry paste
2 tbsp sunflower oil

1 medium onion, sliced thinly
1 garlic clove, crushed
1 tsp ground cumin
1 tsp finely chopped fresh
    ginger root
^{1}/$_2$ tsp chilli paste

4 tsp chicken stock
2 tbsp ground almonds
salt
fresh coriander (cilantro), to garnish

1 Slash the chicken fairly deeply at intervals with a sharp knife and place in a large bowl.

2 Mix together the natural (unsweetened) yogurt and curry paste and stir into the chicken, tossing to coat evenly. Cover and chill for at least 1 hour.

3 Heat the oil in a large pan and fry the onion and garlic for 4–5 minutes until softened but not browned.

4 Stir in the cumin, ginger and chilli paste and cook gently for 1 minute.

5 Add the chicken pieces and fry gently, turning from time to time, for about 10 minutes or until evenly browned. Stir in any remaining marinade with the stock and almonds.

6 Cover the pan and simmer gently for a further 15 minutes or until the chicken is completely cooked and tender.

7 Season to taste with a little salt. Garnish the chicken with coriander (cilantro) and serve with pilau rice, pickles and poppadums.

VARIATION

If you prefer, use boneless chicken breasts instead of legs, and cut into large chunks for cooking.

Cumin-spiced Apricot Chicken

Spiced chicken legs are partially boned and packed with dried apricots for an intense fruity flavour.
A golden, spiced, low-fat yogurt coating keeps the chicken moist and tender.

Serves 4

INGREDIENTS

4 large, skinless chicken
  leg quarters
finely grated rind of 1 lemon
200 g/7 oz/1 cup ready-to-eat
  dried apricots
1 tbsp ground cumin

1 tsp ground turmeric
125 g/4^1/$_2$ oz/^{1}/$_2$ cup low-fat
  natural (unsweetened) yogurt
salt and pepper

TO SERVE:
250 g/9 oz/1^1/$_2$ cups brown rice
2 tbsp flaked (slivered) hazelnuts
  or almonds, toasted
2 tbsp sunflower seeds, toasted
lemon wedges and a fresh salad

1 Remove any excess fat from the chicken legs.

2 Use a small sharp knife to carefully cut the flesh away from the thigh bone.

3 Scrape the meat away down as far as the knuckle. Grasp the thigh bone firmly and twist it to break it away from the drumstick.

4 Open out the boned part of the chicken and sprinkle with lemon rind and pepper. Pack the dried apricots into each piece of chicken. Fold over to enclose, and secure with cocktail sticks.

5 Mix together the cumin, turmeric, yogurt and salt and pepper, then brush this mixture over the chicken to coat evenly. Place the chicken in an ovenproof dish or roasting tin (pan) and bake in a preheated oven, 190°C/375°F/ Gas Mark 5, for about 35–40 minutes, or until the juices run clear, not pink, when the chicken is pierced through the thickest part with a skewer.

6 Meanwhile, cook the rice in boiling, lightly salted water until just tender, then drain well. Stir the hazelnuts and sunflower seeds into the rice. Serve the chicken with the nutty rice, lemon wedges and a fresh salad.

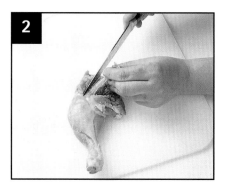

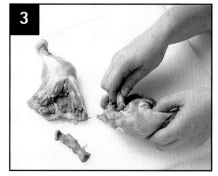

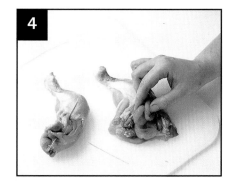

Chilli Coconut Chicken

This tasty Thai-style dish has a classic sauce of lime, peanut, coconut and chilli.
You'll find coconut cream in most supermarkets or delicatessens.

Serves 4

INGREDIENTS

150 ml/^{1}/4 pint/^{2}/3 cup hot
   chicken stock
30 g/1 oz/^{1}/3 cup coconut cream
1 tbsp sunflower oil
8 skinless, boneless chicken thighs,
   cut into long, thin strips

1 small red chilli, sliced thinly
4 spring onions (scallions),
   sliced thinly
4 tbsp smooth or crunchy
   peanut butter
finely grated rind and juice of 1 lime

spring onion (scallion) flower and red
   chilli, to garnish
boiled rice, to serve

1 Place the chicken stock in a measuring jug and crumble the creamed coconut into the stock, stirring to dissolve.

2 Heat the oil in a wok or large heavy frying pan (skillet) and cook the chicken strips, stirring, until golden.

3 Add the sliced red chilli and the spring onions (scallions) to the pan and cook gently for a few minutes, stirring to mix all the ingredients.

4 Add the peanut butter, coconut cream, lime rind and juice and simmer uncovered, stirring, for about 5 minutes.

5 Serve with boiled rice, garnished with a spring onion (scallion) flower and a red chilli.

VARIATION

Serve jasmine rice with this spicy dish. It has a fragrant aroma that is well-suited to Thai-style recipes.

VARIATION

Limes are used frequently in Thai cookery, particularly in conjunction with sweet flavours such as coconut or peanut. They are used in preference to lemons because they have a more acidic flavour which lends freshness and tartness to many dishes. If limes are unavailable, you can use lemons instead.

Index

Index compiled by Lydia Darbyshire